POWER OF A SAINT

KAY D. RIZZO

Pacific Press Publishing Association
Boise, Idaho
Oshawa, Ontario, Canada

"To all who receive Him,
to those who believe in His name,
He gives the power to become a daughter of God."
John 1:12, adapted

Edited by Don Mansell
Designed by Tim Larson
Cover art by Bryant Eastman
Type set in 10/12 Century Schoolbook

Copyright © 1988 by
Pacific Press Publishing Association
Printed in United States of America
All Rights Reserved

Library of Congress Catalog Card Number: 88-61220

ISBN 0-8163-0776-8

Contents

1. Someday I'll Show Them	5
2 Not Good Enough	11
3. The Unwelcome Guest	16
4. Saturday Keeper	21
5. Letter From the States	26
6. Invasion Force	31
7. A Bible and a Doctor	37
8. Evening on the Town	41
9. Escape in the Night	48
10. Uniformed Terror	54
11. A Place of Her Own	58
12. A Stranger in Israel	64
13. A Taste of Heaven	70
14. Friends From Home	76
15. Evening Intruder	81
16. Escape by Fire	86
17. Victory Over Defeat	91

Chapter 1
Someday I'll Show Them

Hate flooded Arturo Sandoval's bearded face as he leaped back from the rough, hand-hewn table to avoid the hot coffee splashing across his plate. With practiced ease, his right hand encircled one end of the heavy sisal rope lying on the floor beside the table. Massive knots segmented the cord every few inches. Evil flashed from beneath his heavy, scowling brows. He moved toward his fifteen-year-old stepdaughter, Flora. A snarl curled his lip. "Stupid, stupid girl! You are a lazy, stupid child."

Frantic, Flora glanced toward the niche in the wall that held a statue of the Virgin Mary, whispering a prayer for protection. Instead of the statue's smiling face, she saw only the vicious whip raised high over Arturo's head. Instinctively, she covered her face and head with her arms as the cord whipped across her shoulders. She screamed in pain and fell to her knees. Over and over again, the whip lashed her slight, quivering body.

"Please stop," she begged, her cries coming in short, painful gasps.

The tropical morning had begun routinely enough. Flora had completed her usual household chores when Doña Alicia, her mother, ordered her youngest daughter to help prepare the *pupusas* (a Salvadoran pastry) her mother would sell in town.

While Arturo, her mother's common-law husband sat at the table, drinking his morning coffee, the girl could feel his brooding stare as she shaped the cornmeal dough into round, flat tortillas. Flora's hands moved skillfully filling one half of the circle with the cheese mixture and folded the empty half of the tortilla over the cheese. As she pinched the corn tortilla edges closed, she tried to think how she could escape.

"Drowning a hangover again, I suppose," Flora mused to herself, "a common ailment for him." Since her mother was in an equally vile mood, the girl worked quickly and quietly.

A brooding silence filled the stuccoed room. Even the statue of the Virgin Mary in the niche seemed to be holding her breath, waiting for the storm to break. As usual, there was no one to stand up for her. Flora's older brother, Marcos, had already left for work as had Rosa, her older sister. Ana, the oldest of the four children, lived on the other side of San Miguel with her husband.

In the old days Grandma Marta would have been there to intervene or at least to comfort her later. But Grandma had become sick with a jungle fever and died. Mysterious infections and cases of unexplained dysentery were common in the small El Salvadoran community.

"If I hurry I can leave for school before Mama leaves for the market, and maybe—" the girl reasoned.

"Flora," Doña Alicia interrupted her thoughts, "be sure to wash the dishes and the table before you leave this morning."

Flora's shoulders slumped. A sigh of defeat escaped her lips. Doña Alicia draped her multicolored shawl about her shoulders and picked up the heavy basket. Now there'd be no escaping Arturo's wrath.

Her mother had just stepped out into the bright El Salvadoran sunlight when Arturo demanded a second cup of coffee. At the sound of his voice, the girl froze.

"Well, get moving, *estupida*!" he snarled.

Quickly, she grabbed an oversized hot pad from the table, hurried out into the courtyard to the cooking area, and retrieved the coffee pot. When she reentered the house, she avoided glancing at Arturo's sneering face. How she hated that sneer.

Her small brown hands shook as she poured the scalding liquid into his cup. When a drop splashed onto his hand, he grabbed the young girl's wrist. This caused the coffee to spill onto the empty stoneware plate in front of him.

Terrified, Flora backed away. As she moved, she stumbled on a chair leg and dropped the half-filled coffeepot. The dark brown liquid splattered across the earthen floor. Knowing what would come next, Flora raised her hands to her face for protection.

As Arturo reached for his sisal whip, he grabbed a handful of the girl's wild, tangled curls and yanked her across the room, then threw her to the floor.

The cutting lashes pummeled the girl's scarred flesh until her cries changed to bleating whimpers. A smile of satisfaction spread across the man's face. Having proved himself a *macho,* he swaggered out of the tiny, two-room row house.

Her body ached with every move as Flora crawled behind the burlap curtain that partitioned off the sleeping area from the main room. Dropping into the tiny space between two of the sleeping cots, she stared silently at the wooden rafters and dusty red tiles above her head. Her sweat trickled across the blood oozing from the ugly welts on her shoulders and back. Flora sighed and leaned her aching head against the cot.

She would never consider complaining to her mother about the beatings Arturo inflicted since Doña Alicia treated her in a similar fashion. Only her beautiful Grandma Marta would have helped.

"Oh, Grandma," the girl wailed, "why did you leave me?" It seemed so long since her grandmother died, and the beatings had become so regular. She wondered if such treatment was normal. Perhaps it's just a part of being a child. "Perhaps I deserve it," she thought. "Maybe I *am* stupid."

It hadn't always been so. She remembered a time before her mother started attending the witch doctor's meetings and before Arturo moved into the house. Back in those days Doña Alicia hadn't been so angry, so filled with evil. But now, those memories seemed more like a dream than reality.

"I can't stand it. I hate him. And I hate her for keeping him here! I wish my father would come and take me away, far far away," she screamed into a handful of bedding hanging over the side of the cot. Within minutes she exhausted her anger. She struggled to her feet, staggering across the room to the wash basin. She peered into the mirror shard wedged on the wall between two nails. Picking up the family hairbrush, she tried to untangle her waist-length curls matted with moist blood from her back and shoulders. "My Papa, if he knew how they treat me, he'd come and rescue me," she whispered in short staccato gasps. But no matter how hard she wished, her Papa never arrived.

Long before Flora was born, her father, Marcos le Fleur, Jr., the tall, angular son of a French coffee plantation owner, had become enamored with the beautiful thirteen-year-old Alicia. Attracted by the girl's exotic honeydew eyes, a mixture of gold and brown, he arranged to have his father purchase the girl as a temporary wife until he could finish law school. Later, after Marcos passed his bar examinations, his father sent to France for a "proper," upper-class bride, leaving Alicia and their children to fend for themselves—an accepted practice in the village of San Miguel. The problem arose when Flora's mother made the mistake of falling in love with the man.

Six children were born to Marcos and Alicia. Rafael, the oldest, died in infancy from tropical fevers. Then came Ana. A baby girl was the third child, but she died minutes after birth. A son, Marcos III arrived, followed by Rosa and Flora. Their father left for the city and his new wife when Flora was eighteen months old, leaving Alicia, barely more than a child herself with the four children to feed. A severe drought intensified the abandoned family's desperation.

Occasionally over the following years, Marcos would come back to San Miguel to visit his children. During those visits, he had taken a special liking to Flora. Years after he ceased his visits, the child remembered the tall man in white who would bounce her on his knee and take her for walks to the town plaza. But always the man would return to his wife in the city.

And after each visit, the devout Doña Alicia would attend mass and light candles to the saints, praying that they would bring the father of her children back to her permanently.

In order to feed her growing children, Alicia made aprons and sold them in the plaza. When a major economic depression hit the country, Alicia decided to sell *pupusas* instead. Meanwhile her prayers for the return of her husband went unanswered. After one stress-filled visit, Marcos left, never to return. But Doña Alicia continued for months afterward to pray for his return. After a time, she became discouraged.

One day as Alicia wept to a neighbor about her loss, the woman suggested that she visit the powerful witch doctor, Carlotta, who lived nearby. Flora's mother hesitated. She'd heard about the woman's power to cast evil spells.

"Carlotta brought Juan Campos back to Elena, and she brought Tomas back to Noemi," the neighbor woman insisted. "I'm sure she can bring Marcos back to you too." Discouraged and lonely, Alicia decided that her only hope was to go to Carlotta for help.

When Grandma Marta heard of her daughter's plans, she warned of the fearful consequences of visiting the demon-controlled woman. Alicia began attending the daily séances. Occasionally, she dragged a reluctant Flora along.

Five-year-old Flora enjoyed the bus ride and the walk through the cool, canopied jungle beyond the famous *Arbol de Fuego* (fire tree). However, the child feared the wizened old woman, who chanted strange incantations in a high-pitched, crackly voice above her head

One visit the witch predicted, "This child has strong powers. If those powers are developed properly, she can become a wealthy woman one day."

Flora barely listened as the two women discussed her powers. The girl believed she had unusual powers. After all Grandma Marta told her so. Flora's favorite story happened when the little dog, Perlita, fought off four wild dogs and saved her life. "God has a purpose for you," Grandma reminded.

Months passed. The witch doctor tried different kinds of love potions and cast a number of spells for Doña Alicia, yet Marcos did not return. During one visit, as Flora played on the floor at her mother's feet, Carlotta announced that Alicia needed to make Marcos jealous. "You must take another man as your lover. I have just the one for you. His name is Arturo Sandoval."

Without questioning this advice, Doña Alicia agreed. Arturo moved into her small home. None of the children liked the growling, abrasive man, especially when he drank native beer.

A year passed. Still Marcos did not return to Alicia. When Alicia complained to Carlotta, the witch suggested, "The spirits have told me that to bring the father of your children back to you, you must give Flora to Arturo as his common-law wife."

"Flora is only six years old!" Alicia exclaimed. "She has just begun school at the convent."

"The spirits have spoken," Carlotta stated flatly. In desperation Alicia agreed to the plan—to Arturo's delight.

For Flora, however, a light went out inside her. The once vivacious child became a shadow that skittered about the house making herself as inconspicuous as possible. Though she didn't understand what was happening to her, she felt dirty and ugly. An overwhelming sense of guilt grew inside of her, crushing her spirit, her confidence, and her intellect. Learning became impossible. Her attention span shrank. At home, the frightened child seldom spoke above a whisper; in fact, she never spoke unless first spoken to.

The convent school became the only place where Flora felt safe enough to reveal her real self to others. It was the only place she felt safe enough to release the happy little girl imprisoned deep within her bruised mind. No one knew or guessed the abuse she experienced almost daily. As the years passed, the child shifted back and forth between her two personalities.

And now, ten years of shame later, it was only by remembering the convent school that Flora could resist the temptation to curl up into a little ball and sleep the day away.

Flora flinched as she dabbed her cuts with a moist washcloth. As she slipped into her school uniform, she checked to be certain that the plaid jumper with the long-sleeved white blouse covered most of her abrasions. She glanced swiftly toward her face in the mirror then looked away. She hated what she saw.

"Ugly! Stupid! Lazy!" she hissed. "Mama is so beautiful with her smooth, bronze complexion, her beautiful eyes, and finely shaped mouth. Rosa looks just like her. And brother Marcos is tall and handsome like Papa. But me? I am ugly, lazy, and stupid just like Arturo says; just like Mama says."

Flora wrinkled her nose in disgust then dipped her hands into the water. She ran her dripping fingers through her waist-length, dark-brown hair, dividing the bulk of it into three heavy strands then braided them together into one braid. After tying a string around the ends, she tossed the braid over her shoulder.

The gong of the mission bell brought her to life. If she hurried, she could still make it to the school in time for morning prayers. And, if she prayed hard enough, maybe tomorrow would be better. Maybe tomorrow she wouldn't be so lazy and so stupid—and so dirty. And someday, she decided, she'd become a saint like the nuns at the convent. Then she'd no longer be dirty or stupid. She'd never again spill hot coffee on the floor or allow the hated Arturo to touch her. She'd be a saint. She'd wear a spotlessly white robe and feel clean, totally clean. She glanced up at the smiling idol and crossed herself. "Yes, Flora le Fleur will become a nun," she determined as she hurried out onto the street. "I'll show them! I'll show them all!"

Chapter 2
Not Good Enough

Flora gazed with rapt attention while Sister Maria explained the geography of the countries north of El Salvador. As the delicate, round-faced nun glided about the room, Flora was certain that the woman's feet never touched the floor. Flora had never seen any of the sisters eat or drink or even wash their hands. She had come to the conclusion that they never needed to bathe their bodies or wash their spotlessly white gowns. They were true saints, and saints didn't have to do these things.

"A saint," Flora thought, watching every move the woman made. "Can I become a saint too?" As the gentle folds of the nun's robe brushed Flora's arm, the child gasped with delight. She longed to reach out and run the snowy white fabric between her fingers, but she dared not.

Flora thought of the picture on the back of the laundry detergent box and sighed. She pictured every detail of the beautiful bride doll with the golden curls and the white satin gown. Though Flora was uncertain as to what a bride doll might be, she ached to own one. Somehow she understood that the doll represented purity and cleanliness. But the five North American dollars it cost to purchase the doll might as well have been $5,000. When the soap box became empty, Flora tore the picture off of it and placed it in the small wooden jewelry box Grandma Marta had given her. And whenever the little girl felt sad or lonely, she would take the picture out and admire the doll.

Time passed; the picture faded. As Flora's dream of ever owning the doll faded, her desire to become a nun grew. Whenever her mother or Arturo beat her, Flora told herself, "Someday it will be better." Whenever Arturo came to her cot for his nocturnal visitations, the young girl would squeeze her eyes shut and imagine herself gliding through the convent halls, wearing a beautiful white robe—forever beyond his control.

"Someday, someday," she would vow—until his next visit. Then she would lament, "It's impossible. I am too dirty. I will never be clean enough to become a saint."

As the young girl's body matured and she discovered the complexities of womanhood, she grew certain that the nuns at the convent had evolved from a different species of women, totally different from her sisters and her mother and now, even herself. She despaired of ever being like them.

"Flora?" a sharp voice broke into her revery. "Flora, I asked you a question!" Sister Maria scolded.

Flora's face reddened. "Yes ma'am," she answered. "I am sorry. I didn't hear you."

"What is the name of this country?" The nun pointed to a large pink mass of land toward the top of the faded wall map.

"Uh, I'm not sure, Sister Maria," the young girl stammered.

"Canada, Flora, Canada," the woman repeated, her voice edged with impatience. "If you would only pay attention."

Flora smiled weakly and nodded. Suddenly an idea exploded in her head. Why should she wait to enter the convent? Wasn't she old enough now—right now, to begin training? The thought startled her. A smile teased the corners of her often serious face. "Yes," she decided, "after geography class, I'll talk with the Mother Superior."

As the bell rang announcing the end of the class, Flora raced toward Mother Superior's office. Her hand trembled as she timidly knocked on the heavy oak door. At the sound of Mother Superior's voice, Flora's heart skipped a beat.

"Come in," called the elderly woman.

Taking a deep breath, Flora opened the door wide enough to allow her slight body to slip inside the room. The room was barren of decoration except for a large wooden crucifix suspended on the back wall, a massive bookcase along the left wall, and a desk with two heavily carved, high-backed chairs. Sunlight from a tall, arched window on the right side lit Mother Superior's wrinkled face.

The elderly woman looked up from the stack of papers before her and smiled. "Yes, my child?"

Flora straightened her shoulders. "I am here to find out what I must do to take my vows. I want to devote my life fully to God."

Mother Superior sighed, slid her thumb and forefinger beneath the metal rims of her glasses, and pinched the bridge of her nose. "Please, Flora," the woman replied softly, "won't you sit down?"

Eager to please, Flora slid into the chair and folded her hands expectantly on her lap.

The two sat in silence—Flora staring at Mother Superior and Mother Superior staring at the desktop. "Flora, my child," she began, her eyes filled with sadness, "I have felt for a long time that one day you would enter my office and make such a request."

"But how?" the surprised girl sputtered. "I told no one, not my family, nor my friends, nor any of the sisters—no one."

"My child, I have seen you every day for the last nine years. Do you think I did not notice how you linger near the convent long after the other children left for home each day? Do you think I didn't notice how you made yourself indispensable around the convent, daily volunteering to clean the chapel, and how you watch every move the sisters make?" The woman tipped her head to one side. "Of course, I knew. I only expected you to ask sooner, on you last birthday, in fact."

"Oh well, I guess I didn't feel worthy." Flora paused, then hastened to add, "I still don't. But I just kind of hoped there might be something I might do to begin to be worthy to take the veil."

The woman pursed her lips into a tight bow, her brows knitted into a frown. "My child," she began, "do not misunderstand.." She paused as if searching for some inner strength to continue. "You can never qualify to take the vows of a nun."

Flora stared in shocked surprise. Her entire world had vaporized into a puff of smoke from Izalco, the angry volcano behind San Miguel. Her dreams—her goals—her tomorrow—her everything! She struggled to speak, "Never? B-b-b-but why? What have I done?"

The woman shook her head sadly. "Nothing, child. You've been a good girl. But your grades haven't been the best, and you daydream too much."

"Daydream?" questioned Flora to herself. Her listlessness could hardly be called daydreaming. It was more due to a lack of sleep. It had been so long since she'd had a complete night of sleep—and this lack wasn't entirely due to Arturo's nightly visits. It was Carlotta's fault—her curses.

"You have been helpful and cooperative during your years here at the convent. However, I have received reports that you question too much. You ask things you shouldn't ask."

Flora searched the nun's face, trying to understand, to make sense out of her words. "Is it for that reason I will not be allowed to enter the convent?" she asked. "I'll change. I promise I won't ask another question if you just let me join the order."

"I'm afraid that won't be good enough, Flora. A much bigger reason is your mother," the woman continued. "Your father never married your mother. That alone makes you ineligible, I am afraid." Mother Superior eased herself from her chair and walked over to the window. "Your father lives in San Salvador with his legal wife and three children, you know."

Flora bit her lip to keep from fainting. Slowly, the woman turned. "Also, your mother visits the witch doctor, regularly. The church does not condone devil worship of any kind. And since your mother is such a devoted follower of Carlotta's, you are bound to be affected in some way."

"But that's not fair," Flora gasped, staring down at her whitened knuckles. "You can't do this to me. I have dreamed for so long . . ." Flora's ears rang; her head pounded. The room swirled before her eyes as she forced her paralyzed legs to stand. Utter desperation flooded her mind. She threw herself down at Mother Superior's feet and buried her face in the creamy folds of the woman's robe. "Reverend Mother, please, you are my only hope, my only escape."

"I am sorry, child. The convent is not a place of escape—a place to hide." The nun laid her hand on Flora's shoulder. "And I'm afraid we do have policies, and one is we will not accept a bas . . . an illegitimate child," Mother Superior corrected herself, then cleared her throat. "I understand your disappointment."

Mother Superior's suggestion failed to register. "Understand? Understand? How can you possibly understand? You don't! You can't! No one does," Flora wailed. Blindly, the girl struggled to her feet and groped for the door. She pushed the heavy oak door open and ran blindly down the hall.

When she reached the courtyard, the midafternoon recess was

in session. Her friends called for her to join them. Covering her face with her hands, she ran in the opposite direction, toward her favorite hiding place, a large shade tree behind the nuns' living quarters. "Alone," she gasped, "I've got to be alone!" She climbed the tree to the third branch and leaned against its trunk.

Flora stared at the neat, one-story building that housed the nuns, then turned away. "It's not fair!" she screamed, not caring who might hear. "I've tried so hard. It's just not fair. Now, I can never be clean enough, pure enough to become a saint, no matter what I do. God will never accept me. It's just not fair!"

Hurt and angry, Flora stared beyond the rosy-hued convent walls at the town and the jungle beyond. She shook her fist into the air. "God, wherever You are, why are You doing this to me? Mother Mary, why are you letting your Son do this to me?" For the first time, Flora seethed with hatred, first at the God, who would refuse her service because of her mother's sin, second at her mother for bringing Arturo into their home, then at Arturo for the abuse she'd endured. She hated the witch, Carlotta, for her incantations and curses. And last, she hated herself.

"Maybe Mother Superior is right. Maybe it is my fault," she thought. "Maybe God really can't allow someone like me to wear the white robes of a saint."

Flora tore a leaf from the branch and shredded it into confetti-size pieces. "And maybe, just maybe, I don't want to serve a God that doesn't want me!"

It wasn't until the last bell rang and the other students had left the convent grounds that Flora left her perch. Her bruises from the morning's beating and from sitting in one position for so long caused her to walk stiffly toward the front gate. When she passed the nuns walking two by two to the chapel, her face reddened and her eyes filled with tears. "They all know," she thought. "They all know that I am too dirty, too sinful, to join them." Flora turned and fled from the convent grounds.

Once beyond the walls, Flora headed for home, kicking a pebble before her as she walked. "Maybe I'll never come back to school. That would teach them," she mumbled. But even as she spoke, she knew she'd return. The convent was her everything. She had to return.

Chapter 3
The Unwelcome Guest

Flora sighed impatiently and stared into the darkness beside her cot. She could hear the rhythmic sounds of the sleeping household. Her mother's gentle snore, along with Arturo's heavier, raspier breathing drifted into the room where she lay. She heard Rosa moan and her brother Marcos babble incoherently in his sleep. Even the distant rat-tit-tat-tat from the guns of the National Guard and Honduran border patrol in the mountains behind the town caught her attention. She listened and waited.

Flora thought of her nightly visitor—the ghost of Grandma Marta. "I wish she'd get this over with so I could get a decent night's sleep for once." Every night had been the same for the last nine years. First Flora would hear the back door rattle. Then she'd hear the familiar squeak as it opened. The sound of footsteps followed until the familiar entity paused just beyond the burlap curtain. A ghastly white hand would appear. Then the being, wearing a long, pink flannel nightgown with the lacy collar and cuffs would step up to Flora's cot, and the tirade would begin again. Always, the message was the same, and always in Grandma Marta's voice. "Let Carlotta use your powers," it would demand.

Flora remembered the day Carlotta had placed the spell on her. Doña Alicia had met her at the convent gates as the day's classes let out. "Carlotta asked me to bring you to her."

"Me? Go with you to the witch doctor? Why?" The child questioned, her eyes wide with terror. She recalled the earlier trips to the cabin in the jungle, the witch's black beady eyes that pierced through to Flora's very soul. She remembered how the woman rattled out nonsensical phrases in an eerie, high-pitched tone. But most of all, seven-year-old Flora remembered the room beyond the closed door where Carlotta stored her magic objects—the jar of snake fangs, the monkey bones, the dried lizards, toads, and beetles that hung from the ceiling on black threads.

"I have been worried about you," her mother explained. "You don't eat well. You don't speak. You never laugh or sing like other children your age.

"Carlotta says it is because a power deep inside of you is struggling to be free. That is what causes your strange behavior. She says that if you let her train that power, you can become a great witch, greater than she."

"Please, no," Flora begged, her voice trembling with fear. "I don't want to go. When Grandma Marta was living, she told me to stay away from the witch doctor and her evil powers."

Doña Alicia raised her hand threateningly. "You are my daughter. You will do as I say."

Whenever Alicia took Flora to the witch's home, Carlotta's eyes would light up. The witch would cup her long, boney fingers over Flora's head and chant. Then she would say, "This child possesses special powers—mighty powers. I can feel them in my fingertips."

The witch then would squeeze and knead the young girl's head as if selecting a melon at the village market. "Yes, I can feel it; I can see it in her eyes," Carlotta explained. "I like to get them young—before their wills are too set."

Flora remembered her one visit all too well. Reluctantly, the young girl followed her mother to the edge of town. As she stepped onto the pathway leading into the jungle, gentle coolness caressed her face. She glanced up at the canopy of trees and vines overhead. She loved the moist jungle with its broad-leafed plants, ropelike vines, and flashy blossoms of red, orange, and yellow. The flowers' fragrance hung heavily in the jungle's moist, warm air. If she hadn't been heading toward Carlotta's place, the child would enjoy the excursion into the jungle.

The seven-year-old ran to catch up with her mother as she disappeared around a bend in the narrow pathway. Flora rounded the bend as Doña Alicia slipped off her sandals and stepped from the sandy beach into the shallow stream. Flora did the same.

When she reached the other side, Flora spotted the gigantic

orange-red blossoms of the sacred *Arbol de Fuego*, the fire tree, in full bloom. Its branches blazed with their fiery blossoms, as if engulfed in flames. Flora ran to pick one of the flowers. Doña Alicia glanced over her shoulder and spotted the child beneath the tree. "Hurry," she called, "Carlotta is expecting us."

Preferring obedience to punishment, Flora's brain sent the message to her feet to walk, but nothing happened. She could not move. The child scowled, then tried to walk again. Again nothing happened.

"Mama," Flora wailed, "I can't move."

Doña Alicia whirled around, her multicolored skirt whipping about her ankles like a matador's cape. "I said to come!"

Tears spilled down Flora's cheeks. "Honest, Mama. I really can't move my feet."

Impatient, the woman stormed back to where the child stood and yanked at Flora's sleeve. "You come with me now, or I am going to whip you good!" she threatened. "I'll have Arturo use his whip on you too."

The child looked up into her mother's agitated face. "Mama, you can do whatever you want to me, but I cannot go with you. My feet won't move."

Doña Alicia raised her hand to slap her daughter's face, then froze. For no apparent reason, the woman's arm dropped uselessly to her side. Consternation replaced her anger. "Fine. You wait right here for me. Don't you dare move until I return," she growled as she stomped down the pathway.

Once her mother disappeared from view, Flora's feet and legs could move again. To be certain everything was working properly, the girl jumped, kicked, and hopped about in a circle beneath the tree. Relieved, she sat down beneath the tree to wait for her mother's return.

And now, so many years later, Flora remembered. She remembered all too well, even the conversation she overheard that night between her mother and Arturo.

"It was the strangest thing," her mother explained. "The child actually could not move her feet."

Arturo snorted in disgust. "She was defying you. You should have forced her to obey."

"No, I could tell by the look in her eyes that what she told me was true," Doña Alicia replied. "The strange part was when I arrived at the cabin, Carlotta was standing in the doorway, staring into the jungle. She barely acknowledged my arrival though she was looking straight at me." Alicia's voice dropped to a whisper.

Laying on her cot beyond the sleeping curtain, Flora strained to catch every word.

"Before I could explain Flora's absence, Carlotta described in detail the entire event, about stopping beneath the *Arbol de Fuego*, about Flora's not being able to move—our entire conversation. Then she said it was better that Flora remain by the tree. She actually told me Flora's powers kept her own from working properly," Doña Alicia admitted. "I don't know what to make of it."

"Bah!" Arturo growled. "Just a bunch of mumbo jumbo."

"Arturo," Doña Alicia argued, "she says that Flora could become a rich woman one day, if she'd only allow herself to be trained properly in the use of those powers."

"So train her!" Arturo snorted. "Let her put food in our bellies and fancy clothes on our backs."

"Thanks to my mother, Flora refuses to cooperate," Alicia complained.

"Well, I know how to make the kid cooperate."

"I don't think you do," Alicia warned. "Flora's a lot stronger than she looks. Carlotta also predicted that one day Flora would fly on a giant bird to a country far from here and once there, she'd fall in love with a man from another country."

"Fairy tales!"

"No, Arturo, listen. Carlotta is determined to break the child's resistance. And we are to help her," Doña Alicia continued. "She's cast a spell on the child. The spell has something to do with my mother."

Flora shuddered and snuggled down under her blanket until only her large, brown eyes and the top of her head remained visible.

Nine long years had passed, and Flora still remembered every word her mother had said. And every night since then the apparition garbed in Grandma Marta's favorite nightgown had appeared, argued, and taunted the child.

When she heard the doorknob rattle, Flora squeezed her eyes shut. She felt the being's presence before she saw it. A smothering heaviness pervaded the atmosphere in the room.

"Hello, Flora," the apparition greeted. "I see you are waiting for me."

"Go away," the girl whispered.

The being shook its head sadly. "As I've told you so many times before, I want to but I can't until you cooperate with Carlotta. I am in limbo. I will not rest in the Eternal Kingdom until you submit," she said. "I know how you have suffered at your parents' hands. Let Carlotta help you. She can release the power within you that will give you control over your enemies."

"No, no I can't," Flora argued. "You yourself warned me against trusting Carlotta. You said the saints would be angry if I did."

The form smiled tenderly, reached out and stroked the young girl's forehead. "I know, child, but I was wrong."

Flora turned away from the ghostly visitant and buried her head in her pillow. "I-I-I can't," she sobbed.

"You have to; you must!" the being snarled in a raspy voice, totally out of character with Grandma Marta's high, lilting tones.

"Go away," Flora cried.

At the sound of her own voice, the light vanished. Flora clutched herself to control her trembling body. As always, she felt feverish, yet chilled; her stomach was knotted with pain; her lightweight blanket had twisted about her legs.

Flora's prayer came in short gasps. "Oh Mary, mother of Jesus," she pleaded. Crossing herself automatically, she prayed the prayer she'd learned at the convent. And from its niche in the wall, the brightly painted plaster figurine neither heard nor supplied an escape from the forces of evil attacking her defenses.

Chapter 4
Saturday Keeper

"Flora, hurry. I've got something to tell you. You will never believe it. Hurry." Marietta danced about as Flora approached the convent gates minutes before the first bell rang.

Flora waved and broke into a trot. "What are you so excited about so early in the day?" Flora asked her friend. "A new boyfriend?"

"No, of course not," Marietta answered, blushing at the thought. "Mama would never—"

"Well then, what is the matter?" Flora asked as the two girls entered the convent doors.

"We are to have a man teacher—for math! Can you believe it? A man?" Marietta giggled. "The only man ever allowed in the convent is Father Fuentes when he comes to teach the catechism classes!"

At the mention of his name, a shiver of fear ran the length of Flora's spine. She cringed every time she stepped into the old priest's classroom—partly because he wore black, but mostly because he was a man, and she hated men. "You've got to be kidding! How? Why?" she asked, half expecting her friend's tale to be another joke.

"I'm serious," Marietta insisted. "On Friday, Sister Lucia transferred to a convent in Nicaragua. So the National Director of Education sent Señor Ortega from San Salvador to substitute until a qualified, permanent teacher can be found."

"Is he young?" Flora whispered, her eyes darting from side to side, not wanting anyone to hear her.

Marietta snickered. "Of course not. He's ancient—at least forty, I'd say. He's short, not much taller than I am, and he's going bald!"

"This I've gotta see." Flora led the way to the science and

mathematics classroom. From half way down the hall, she could hear her classmates' excited voices. When she stepped into the room, she was disappointed to discover that the cause of the disruption hadn't appeared yet. She and Marietta quickly took their seats in the second row.

Carmen, a tall, pimply girl with horn-rimmed glasses preened herself. "I saw him go into Mother Superior's office," she announced, her shoulders sashaying slightly.

Elena, the class mischief maker, grinned. "I think we should give him a hard time."

"Yeah," the group chorused.

"What could we do?" Marietta asked, her pretty face wrinkling into a scowl.

Angelita, the most studious of the group, suggested, "We could switch names when he calls roll."

The girls stared in surprise at the source of the suggestion.

"Yeah," Elena agreed, "that's a great idea. Everyone take the name of the one sitting to your left."

Approaching footsteps ended the conversation. When Mother Superior and the substitute teacher entered the classroom, all seventeen girls cast wide-eyed, angelic smiles their way.

Mother Superior scowled for a moment, then stepped behind teacher's desk. "Young ladies, I'd like your attention please," she began. "This is Señor Ortega. He will be teaching all of Sister Lucia's classes. I expect you to give him the respect you give your other teachers. And now," the woman paused," I will call roll and introduce each of you to him." As Mother Superior looked down to read the roster, the girls groaned. After the last name was called, Mother Superior nodded to the students and the teacher, then left the room.

As the nun disappeared down the hall, the slight, balding gentleman cleared his throat. "I understand Sister Lucia completed chapter 12 in your math book. So today I will introduce factoring." Señor Ortega began writing numbers on the blackboard. By the end of class, Flora had to admit Señor Ortega knew his math and knew how to make it almost understandable.

Before too many days had passed, the students had learned much about their new teacher. A number of the students, including Flora, managed to stay after class to hear more about his life in the big city.

By Friday, Flora knew Señor Ortega rode back and forth by bus each day, that he had a wife and five children, and that he was on loan from the University of El Salvador.

When Angelita asked what he and his family might do on weekends, Señor Ortega answered, "Tomorrow, we'll go to church, and on Sunday, my wife and I will take the children to the mountains."

The girls glanced at one another. Elena, the least reserved, asked, "Saturday? You go to church on Saturday?"

"Yes," he answered. Then quickly turning his attention to the open math book on his desk, he said, "You say you had trouble with problem fifteen?"

"But everyone goes to church on Sunday," Flora blurted before thinking.

Señor Ortega looked up from the textbook. His eyes twinkled as if he was hiding an exciting secret. "Not me nor my family," he said, "and a number of other people, I might add."

"That's impossible!" Marietta huffed. "I never heard of such a thing."

Señor Ortega pursed his lips and asked, "Didn't you girls know that Jesus, the Son of God, attended church on Saturday?"

Flora gasped, "Oh! I can't believe you said that! That's, that's blasphemy!"

"I didn't say it; the Bible says it," Señor Ortega replied, feigning innocence in every word.

Flora scowled and edged closer. "How do you know that? You can't read the Bible. Only the priests are allowed to read the Bible. Only saints can interpret its meaning," she insisted.

Señor Ortega smiled and pointed his finger at the outraged girl. "You're partly right. Only saints can understand the Word of God. That's why I own a Bible; I am a saint." A series of gasps swept about the room.

"Oh, Señor Ortega, don't say that," Flora begged. "The sisters will never let you stay if you make such outrageous claims."

"I'll tell you what, Flora," he began, "on Monday, I will prove to you that I am a saint and that I can read the Bible and understand its teachings. I will even show you where it says that we should worship on Saturday, OK?"

Like a shot, the girls rushed en masse from the classroom. Horrified, yet more than a little captivated by the thought of disobeying convent rules, the girls made a pact to tell no one of Señor Ortega's blasphemous remarks until after he presented his so-called proofs on Monday.

Throughout the rest of Friday, Flora couldn't keep her mind on her classes. At home, Alicia slapped her daughter's face, when she failed to fill the water pot for washing the dishes.

On Saturday as Flora washed her two school uniforms and hung them out to dry, she tried to imagine Señor and Mrs. Ortega and their children sitting in a church somewhere in the capital city. Whenever she remembered his claim of being a saint, she crossed herself, praying he be forgiven for his sin.

As she knelt at mass on Sunday morning, Flora studied the images lining the walls of the chapel. She remembered her teacher's words, "I am a saint" and shuddered. Saint Anthony appeared more grim than usual. Saint Peter and Saint Francis looked angry also. She wished she had some coins to light a candle for her new friend.

On Monday, Flora and her friends could hardly wait until the bell announced the end of math class so they could hear and see Señor Ortega's proof.

"First, about worshiping on Saturday," he said reaching into his leather briefcase and drawing out a large black book. "In Exodus 20, right here, see? Read it aloud, Flora." He handed the girl his book.

Her hands shook as she took the Bible from Señor Ortega. She almost expected to be zapped by lightning because of her audacity. Her brown eyes widened in fear as she began reading where he'd indicated. "Remember the Sabbath day to keep it holy...." Before she concluded the passage, Marietta raced across the room to the giant wall calendar and counted off the days.

"Sunday, Monday," Marietta continued until she came to Saturday," and Saturday is the seventh day—one, two, three, four, five, six, seven! It's not possible!" The other girls clustered around Marietta, each counting for herself the seven-day cycle.

"Then why don't most people go to church on Saturday?" Carmen demanded.

"A long time ago, a Roman emperor changed the day of worship from Saturday to Sunday. It is a long story, but before I share it with you, I want to prove to you that I really am a saint and you can be too." He took the Bible from Flora and leafed through the well-worn pages, reading verse after verse that spoke about the saints as God's children. "How about this one in Ephesians 2:10, 18, 19? For we are His workmanship, created in Christ Jesus unto good works, which God hath before ordained that we should walk in them." "For through Him we both have access by one Spirit unto the Father. Now therefore ye are no more strangers and foreigners, but fellowcitizens with the saints, and of the household of God." Señor Ortega paused a moment, then repeated, " 'Fellow citizens, created in Christ Jesus, saints, able to talk directly to the Father.' Do you understand what that means?"

The girls silently struggled with this new idea.

"It means, as a saint, I can talk directly to the Father in heaven. I don't need to pray to Mary or to any other being, alive or dead," Señor Ortega explained. "And you, Flora, I think you will appreciate this verse—Revelation 19:8."

He read the words aloud. " 'To her was granted that she should be arrayed in fine linen, clean and white; for the fine linen is the righteousness of saints."

Flora eyed the strange little man. How could he know her dream to one day wear the pure white robe of the saints? Her face reddened, certain everyone could read her thoughts.

A longing to have a Bible of her own surged through her. "Señor Ortega," she measured her words, "I would like to have a Bible, to study for myself." The other girls started in surprise.

"I wish I could get one for you," he said, shaking his head sadly, "but Bibles are very, very expensive." He paused a moment. "However, as long as I am allowed to teach at this school, I will hand copy the Scriptures for you. Would you like that?"

Flora nodded enthusiastically. "Señor," she whispered, "would you copy off what you read in Revelation for me?"

Señor Ortega's face wreathed with happiness. "I'll have it for you first thing tomorrow morning," he answered.

Flora walked silently from the classroom. Could this be true? Could what Señor Ortega read be a trick or a lie? Would God listen to her prayers directly? Questions swirled through her brain faster than she could handle them. Could it be the nuns were no more saintly than she, herself, might become—just ordinary women dressed in pretty white robes? When Flora reached the convent gates, she walked rapidly toward home, hoping to outdistance the confusion she felt.

Chapter 5
Letter From the States

Flora ran the dish towel over the last dish from breakfast and placed it on the upturned wooden crate that served as a cupboard. She loved the peace of the empty house. A smile spread across her face as she thought about the things she'd learned from the Bible that week. "A saint, I can be a saint."

Señor Ortega had kept his word. Each evening he copied long passages of Scripture for the eager students.

Flora's excitement grew with each new truth.

"Flora," Señor Ortega confided one day after class, "I have a special text written out especially for you. Did you know that God wants you to be His very own daughter? It's recorded in John 1:12." He handed her a folded piece of paper.

Flora's eyes widened with surprise. "Me? His daughter?" With trembling hands, she opened the paper and read, " 'But as many as received him, to them gave he power to become the daughters of God, even to them that believe in his name.' "

"A daughter of God? A real daughter—with a real Father!" The thought wound itself around her imagination.

At home that night, she read the text many times before placing it in the small wooden jewelry box she stored beneath her sleeping cot. Flora schemed to receive Señor Ortega's hand-copied Scriptures last after all the other girls finished reading them. Now Flora's box bulged with the treasured missives. Only a stout rubber band held the cover securely in place.

One Friday after classes, Flora sneaked into the secluded garden behind the nuns' living quarters. She'd decided to find out for herself if the sisters were somehow different from other humans, or if Mr. Ortega was right, that anyone could become a saint.

Tucking her skirts carefully around her legs, she scampered up the tree to her favorite branch. Before long a group of sisters appeared behind one of the large arched windows. Flora gaped in astonishment when they sat at the table and ate tortillas with frijoles. She'd never seen them eating, especially the everyday food she ate. Flora continued to watch even after the women left the dining room. Before long, she spied Sister Maria in one of the second-floor windows. Flora watched as the nun removed her wimple and brushed her short-cropped hair.

"They are people—just like me," Flora suppressed a squeal of delight, as she scrambled down from the tree. "Señor Ortega and the Bible must be right. I can be a saint too."

The weekend seemed interminable to the eager Flora. Even the four-hour martial law the National Guard declared on Sunday afternoon didn't dampen her enthusiasm. After all, such curfews were a regular occurrence in her town while her discovery that she might be a saint was a once-in-a-lifetime dream come true.

Flora could hardly wait to tell Señor Ortega the good news. On Monday morning, she hurried through her chores and slipped out of the house before Doña Alicia realized she'd left.

From the moment, she entered the convent grounds, Flora sensed something was wrong. She hurried to find Marietta.

Marietta, her temper flaring from every pore, met Flora at the classroom door. "Señor Ortega is gone," she growled, "somebody squealed about the Bible. They won't let him come back."

"What?" Flora blanched. "Who would tell?"

"I don't know," Marietta huffed. "Maybe someone passing in the hall heard us talking."

Never seeing the kind, gentle Christian again, never being allowed to read from the Scriptures made Flora feel faint. She'd just accepted it, only to have it snatched from her.

"I guess we did get pretty careless," Marietta admitted.

Flora slammed her books onto the desktop with unaccustomed force.

"I'm going to see Mother Superior right away. She can't do this to us or to Señor Ortega."

Marietta extended her arm across the classroom door. "You can't. Mother Superior went to the plaza this morning."

Flora thought for a moment, then removed her friend's arm from the doorjamb saying, "I'll see Father Fuentes instead."

Marietta's eyes widened. "You? You'll go to see the priest?"

"Absolutely!" Without thought of consequence, Flora stormed from the room and down the hall to the parish priest's study. She barely knocked on the door before bursting into the office.

The white-haired priest looked up from his desk. "I need to talk to you about one of the teachers," Flora began.

"You should speak with Mother Superior," he said, nodding slightly. "She is in charge of our teaching staff."

"No, I must talk to you," she insisted. Before the priest could react, she continued, "Why did you let Señor Ortega go?"

The man's lips narrowed into paper-thin creases. His eyes smoldered as he spoke. "From what I understand, you know the reasons very well. The man is a heretic!" He pounded his fist on the desk. "How he ever got assigned to our school. . . ! The authorities are supposed to screen . . . !"

The priest stopped midsentence. "Just one moment. I don't have to explain anything to you. Who do you think you are, bursting into my office and questioning my judgment?"

"I am a saint, a full-fledged saint. And thanks to Señor Ortega, I now know it!" Flora answered, her chin jutting defiantly forward. "Rules and regulations would not allow me to become a nun. I was not good enough! But God says I can be a saint just like Peter and John and—and even Paul." Determination flashed from her eyes. "The Bible says that someday, Jesus will take me to live with Him, and He'll give me a beautiful robe of pure white to wear, purer than anything the sisters wear too."

The old priest grabbed for his throat. "Young lady, you are uttering blasphemy!"

"And one day," she continued, "I will have a Bible of my own. I will read every word." Her anger spent, Flora's knees began to quiver. A wave of nausea swept over her as she realized the seriousness of what she'd done.

Flora waited until after the priest had spoken again. "Child, you are overwrought. You must understand the Bible was given to the priests to interpret for the common people. I, myself, have one and can understand its passages, for I am ordained of God." His condescending tones rekindled her courage.

A smile broke on Flora's sun-bronzed face. It was as if she'd willed him to make such a claim. "If you understand the Bible so well," she challenged, "tell me what Exodus 20:8 means? Señor

Ortega knows. So do I."

The priest's face hardened. "Leave my office and these holy grounds—*now!*" he ordered. "Go home and pray for your soul."

"Yes, sir!" Flora responded proudly. "I will pray for my soul—and yours too." Whirling about, she marched from the room.

Her anger sustained her until she reached the street. Suddenly she realized that the convent, her only safe haven, was now forever closed to her. She had no place to go but home.

Questions flooded Flora's mind. "How could Father Fuentes do such a thing? How could the God Señor Ortega worships so faithfully allow such a thing to happen? Doesn't God know how much I need Señor Ortega? Doesn't He realize how much I want to learn? Doesn't He want me and my friends to find Him?"

Flora kicked a pebble into the drainage ditch by the road. She kicked another and another until her shoes bore several layers of dust. "I'll work in the stall selling Mama's *pupusas*," she decided, "I'll work there during the day, then come home and clean the house at night. Mama will be happy for my help."

Later when she told her mother about leaving school, Flora waited for the first blow to fall, but none came. Doña Alicia ranted about the room, banging pots and pans and slamming the door. Arturo stormed from the house, saying he was going to get drunk, but no one asked why she left school.

By the time Flora crawled under her blanket for the night, she wasn't so sure even she cared anymore. Tears swam before her eyes as she let go of her dream to become a nun. As the tears trickled down her cheeks, she wiped them on the sleeve of her nightgown. "School's in the past; so is religion, at least until I can get a Bible and learn for myself."

When Carlotta's spirits visited her bedside that night, Flora ignored them. She had bigger problems to think about.

Starting early the next morning, Doña Alicia kept her busy every minute of the day, and often late into the night. Flora grieved as her friends passed the house on their way to school.

The evening of her sixteenth birthday, Flora arrived home from the plaza to find all of her belongings packed into a suitcase, sitting in the center of the room. "Mama, what is this?" she asked. "What is happening?"

"It is quite simple," her mother began. "You are sixteen now, old enough to care for yourself. When I was your age, I had two children. You're not even courting yet. I have decided there is no longer room for you here."

Flora struggled to comprehend the meaning of her mother's words. She glanced toward the sneering Arturo seated off to one corner. She looked about for help, but none was forthcoming. Her brother Marcos sat with his face hidden behind a newspaper. "Rosa," Flora thought, "where is Rosa? Surely she would help me." But Rosa was not at home. Flora grabbed hold of the chair back to steady herself.

"I have received a letter from my sister, Carmelita," Doña Alicia explained. "She works as a maid in Los Angeles, California. She wants me to send you to her." The woman turned and walked out to the cooking area behind the house. Flora followed.

"Mama, I don't want to go away. What have I done to displease you? Tell me and I'll change. Do you want me to work harder? I'll do more," she pleaded. "Whatever it is, I'll change. Please, don't send me away." Doña Alicia frowned and turned away.

"This isn't happening—it can't be happening!" Flora clutched her arms and rocked silently to ease the pain. "You would send me away? I don't even know Aunt Carmelita. Where is this place called California?

Doña Alicia grasped the handle to the skillet of refried beans and returned to the house. "You have until morning to decide what to do."

During the night, the witch's curse scolded Flora, "She's getting rid of you because you refuse to obey. Maybe it isn't too late."

"No, no! I won't listen to you," Flora buried her face in her pillow."

"Go to your mother and ask her to take you to Carlotta. Maybe Carlotta can change her mind."

"No, no! I can't give in to Carlotta," Flora whimpered. "I just can't."

The evil spirit sneered, "Where's that so called Invisible Power now? What good has it done you to keep it to yourself? Did it come to your aid at the convent school? Will it change your mother's mind?"

Flora tossed about on her cot until shades of pink and gold streaked the sky. Finally she fell into a fitful sleep. When she awakened, Flora tried to convince herself it had all been a bad dream.

Chapter 6
Invasion Force

"You either go to the United States or stay in El Salvador. It's up to you. But if you stay here, leave this house," Said Doña Alicia matter-of-factly, shrugging her shoulders disinterestedly.

Without a word, Flora submerged the iron frying pan and spatula into the hot sudsy dishwater and began scrubbing. A gust of hot air burst through the front door as Rosa strolled in. She walked silently to the table and sat down. Flora sensed that Rosa already knew about the letter and Alicia's decree. She looked to Rosa then to Marcos for support. They avoided her gaze. She turned once more to her mother. "Mama, I will work for you. I will do everything you ask. I will be so good you will hardly know I'm here."

Doña Alicia glanced down at her sobbing daughter. "Your tears will not help. You cannot live here any longer. I have made up my mind."

"Mama," Marcos interrupted, eyeing Flora thoughtfully before speaking, "All night I have been thinking and have come to a decision. If Flora does not wish to go to the United States, I would. There is nothing for me here in El Salvador," he admitted. "Our government is politically unstable and on the verge of war. These border skirmishes can't remain skirmishes forever. The drought shows no sign of stopping, so there's no work on the plantations." The young man folded and unfolded his large brown hands as he spoke. "In this country, I will never be able to own anything more than the shirt on my back. I have nothing to lose by leaving. There, at least, if I work hard, I have a chance." He glanced toward his mother standing at the far end of the table.

"Do as you wish," Doña Alicia shrugged. "But Flora still must leave this house!"

"I know, mother," Marcos replied. "I agree it would be best for Flora to get away from here." He took Flora's hand tenderly. "That's why I left the house early this morning to visit Ana and Juan. With Ana pregnant, Juan could use your help in his print shop at least until the baby comes," he explained. "Later, you can work something else out perhaps."

Flora thought about her sister and her sister's husband, Juan. She didn't feel comfortable around Juan. Yet the idea of working in the print shop appealed to her more than moving to America. "Oh, Marcos, you have saved my life. I am so grateful to you." She threw her arms around his neck and kissed his cheek.

"Hey, you're doing me the favor, Little One." Marcos beamed with happiness. "I get to take Aunt Carmelita up on her offer and go in your place."

Suddenly Flora stopped, her face distorted with pain. "Will I ever see you again Marcos?"

"Who's to know? Maybe one day you will decide to go to the United States also."

"Me? Never!" Flora declared, her eyes flashing with determination.

Before Flora could change her mind, Marcos left for the United States and she found herself at Ana and Juan's home on the opposite side of town. Their home and print shop shared a building with a medical clinic run by Dr. and Señora Diaz from Mexico. Flora learned how to set type, operate the printing press, and ward off Juan's unwelcome advances. Because of her uneasy status in the home, Flora often found herself alone—and lonely. And from the letters received from Marcos who had found work in a far-off place called New York City, she knew he was lonely too. One of his letters read:

> Cold most of the time. They say that the weather improves in May or June. Well, we shall see.
> Money doesn't grow on trees in this country. One has to work hard for every colón (I should say dollar) earned, but at least I have found work. My job washing dishes in a small Spanish restaurant on East Side pays for my room.

To think that I, Marcos le Fleur, would one day do women's work to survive!

Juan, the owner of the restaurant where I work, allows me to eat leftovers each night. So I eat better than you do. (A tortilla and a scoop of beans do not fill the belly, as you know.)

I read in the papers that the war has escalated. My friend Pepe keeps me informed. He rents a room on the next floor down—parents live in San Salvador, and they send him the San Salvadoran newspaper. I will never return to my country and I miss you, Little One.

Flora sniffed as she reread Marcos's letter. She missed him too. He had been her only ally during her later growing up years. She wondered why Marcos left Aunt Carmelita's place in warm California to live all alone in a frigid climate like he described.

She sighed and reached down to pet Chiquita, the family's pet mongrel, who'd appointed himself as her protector. Every day, the situation grew more difficult inside the print shop. Juan's persistence had escalated during the last few weeks. One night he sneaked into Flora's small bedroom. She had pretended to be asleep. A growl from Chiquita, sleeping under Flora's bed, deterred him. From then on, Flora always checked before closing her bedroom door making sure Chiquita was by her side.

The situation outside the print shop intensified also. Flora didn't need the San Salvadoran newspapers to tell her how the war was going. The sound of rifle fire and machine guns could be heard in the distance most any hour of the day. She shivered when she overheard Dr. Diaz and Juan talking one afternoon. "The print shop and medical clinic will be a prime target for the enemy," the doctor confided. Juan agreed.

Martial law became as common as wash day in the small town. Whenever the army jeeps rolled into town and the bullhorn roared, Flora would run through the shop, barring doors and windows. Then they would huddle beneath a massive mahogany table used for collating printed materials until the army sounded an all-clear. An alert might last several minutes or a number of hours. And with each, the civilians never knew whether the alert was a practice or if enemy soldiers were attacking the town. One could be shot on sight if caught outside during the curfew.

Early one evening, Ana and Juan went to visit friends. Flora was working folding some pamphlets Juan needed to deliver the next morning. Suddenly she heard the jeeps blaring horns and the official announcement.

Out of habit, she dropped the heavy bar into place on the door and secured the window shutters, then crawled beneath the table. Chiquita nestled close to Flora.

"Don't worry, Chiquita," she soothed. "It will be over soon."

Flora listened to the rata-tat-tat of machine guns. Instinctively she realized that this alert was not a practice. She cringed as rifle bullets whined past the front door. At any moment, she expected to see the door burst open and enemy soldiers barge in and open fire.

"Oh, mi Dios, wherever You are," she prayed, "if you are as real as Señor Ortega promised, and if I can talk to You without talking to Mother Mary first, hear my prayer."

Flora had long ago decided to stop praying to plaster-of Paris saints. She asked for the Power's protection, crossing herself at the end of her prayer.

The fighting continued throughout the night and into the next day. When she heard a body thud against the front door, Flora hugged the excited dog to her chest. She could hear the injured soldier moaning but dared not open the door to him. With the high-pitched whistle from each cannon ball, she tensed, expecting the clinic to burst apart in a ball of fire at any moment. Nearby explosions rained debris against the side of the building.

For hours she sat in total darkness. She didn't dare leave the protection of the table. Her leg muscles cramped from her confinement. She wiggled her feet in order to awaken them from their prickly sleep.

Exhaustion overpowered Flora's fears as she tipped her head forward onto the sleeping pup. Suddenly she heard a scraping sound moving along the inner wall separating the print shop from the clinic. Icy needles tingled within the base of her skull.

At the peak of the open-beamed ceiling there was a space that allowed ventilation for both the clinic and the print shop. Someone was trying to enter the print shop through that space.

Suddenly the scratching stopped. A man spoke, barely above a whisper. "Hola! Anybody here?"

Flora's breath caught in her throat. She squeezed Chiquita

tighter, clamping the dog's jaws shut so he could not bark at the intruder.

"Juan? Ana? Flora? Are you in there?" the man asked, his voice filled with urgency. "It is I, Dr. Diaz. I have a way of escape. But we must leave at once."

Flora held her breath. Could she believe the man? What if it were a trick? Then again, what other choice did she have? Chiquita squirmed, trying to break free from her grasp, causing Flora's arm to bump a chair leg.

"Hola! Who is down there?" Dr. Diaz called. "Answer me, please!"

"It's me," Flora whispered. "I'm under the table."

"The Hondurans are planning to bomb the clinic tonight. My wife and I are leaving for our cabin in the mountains," he added. "My Puegeot is parked at the edge of town. We have room to take you too."

"Can Chiquita come too?"

"Of course," the doctor assured her. "Chiquita is also welcome. Hand her to me, but we must hurry."

Flora crawled out from under the table and stretched. Holding Chiquita in one arm, she pushed the heavy mahogany table up against the wall, planted a straight-back chair on top and climbed up. Immediately, large hands encircled the dog's belly, lifting it over the wall.

"Now it's your turn," Dr. Diaz encouraged.

The stygian darkness exaggerated the distance over the wall. Flora's feet slipped repeatedly off the rough adobe bricks. She was relieved when she reached for another hand hold to discover the smooth wooden beam.

Hoisting her legs over the wall, she felt Dr. Diaz's strong hands encircle her waist and lower her to the floor. Another high-pitched whistle sent Dr. Diaz and Flora running blindly across the room. He guided her to a small doorway. Chiquita bounded after them. In a corner of a bedroom, Mrs. Diaz and the five Diaz children waited.

Dr. Diaz explained their escape. "Everyone join hands. We're going down into the cold-storage room beneath the clinic. There's a side exit into an alleyway behind the building."

Forming a single line with Flora and Chiquita anchoring, they stepped gingerly down the stairs.

"When I open this door, we won't talk again until we're beyond the city limits. Once we leave the clinic, don't let go of anyone's hand until we reach the car," the man ordered. "Move as quietly as you can. Flora, if we get separated, head into the jungle and hide as best you can until we find you. Do you understand?"

"Yes," whispered Flora, her teeth chattering from fear. She wiped her clammy hands on her wrinkled skirt and grasped one of the children's hand.

"All right—ready? Here goes." the doctor opened the narrow door. The smoke-laden night air cast an eerie haze over the fugitives as they crept silently down the street toward the edge of town.

As a jeep's headlights approached, Dr. Diaz leaped into a narrow alley. They all flattened themselves against a building. The vehicle stopped in the middle of the intersection while one of the soldiers flashed a beam of light up and down the garbage-strewn alley.

Flora fought the urge to run, run as fast as she could—away from the soldiers—but managed to hold fast to the young boy's hand ahead of her and hoped the group wouldn't be discovered. Though it seemed like hours to the eight fugitives, in a matter of seconds the jeep drove on. Immediately Dr. Diaz was on the run again, hauling his string of charges behind him. When they reached the edge of town, they crossed a carefully manicured lawn, shinned up a stone wall, and dropped to the jungle floor beyond. After another short run, they crowded into the waiting automobile. With one child perched on each knee, Flora leaned her head against the seat's cool vinyl interior. She could hear Chiquita in the trunk, searching for a comfortable spot in which to lie down. Exhausted from their adventure, the two children soon leaned against her and fell asleep.

Chapter 7
A Bible and a Doctor

Flora paced the wide veranda of Dr. Diaz's country home. Two days had passed since she fled from her sister Ana's home. The cannons and machine-gun fire had ceased echoing up the mountain passes for more than twenty-four hours. She sighed impatiently and glanced down at the youngest of the Diaz children playing in the sand, then toward the horizon. The sun would disappear soon. Dr. Diaz had gone to check on the clinic around daybreak and hadn't returned.

When Mrs. Diaz called the children into the house to prepare for bed, Flora scooped the little boy into her arms and carried him to his mother. Helping the children prepare for bed helped Flora forget her uneasiness. She was picking up the last of the soiled play clothes when she heard the approaching Peugeot. Tossing the clothing into the hamper, she ran to the front door.

The short, rotund doctor bounded from the car, his face beaming with happiness. "Everyone into the car," he announced. "We can go home. The fighting has stopped and curfew has been lifted."

While Dr. and Mrs. Diaz rounded up the children and their belongings, Flora grabbed the dog and ran to the waiting car. Within minutes they were back home, sharing their adventures with Ana and Juan.

Ana told of their two days at their friends' house unable to go outside, adding, "We had no choice but to stay, once martial law was declared. I am so glad Dr. Diaz helped you."

"It's a miracle the clinic and print shop are still standing. A few things are missing from my medical cabinet, but, all in all, everything is in good condition," Dr. Diaz added.

"They didn't touch anything in the print shop," Juan added. "It's business as usual tomorrow."

Two days later, Doña Alicia appeared at the shop unannounced. She greeted her eldest daughter with an embrace. "I am so glad to see that you are all right," she said. "I worried about you and my first grandchild." She patted Ana's protruding stomach tenderly. "I would like to speak with you alone, please." She immediately led the way toward the family's living quarters. Ana followed. Flora shrugged at her mother's lack of greeting and returned to her work.

Before long, Ana tapped Flora on the shoulder. "Mama wants to talk with you."

"Me?" Flora thought. "Whenever she wants to talk to me, it means trouble." The girl reluctantly followed Ana into the parlor.

"Flora, I have received another letter from Carmelita requesting I send you to her. But, of course, you are not smart enough to go, are you?" Doña Alicia sneered. "If you worked at her place, you could be of value to the family by sending your wages back here to help me, but will you do it? Hmmph!"

Flora cleared her throat, hoping for time to think of the right words to say. But no words came. She stood a moment, staring at her mother as if she were a stranger.

That night, Mama's words haunted Flora far more than the witch doctor's spirits. "Is Mama right? Should I accept Aunt Carmelita's offer this time? I'm sure Marcos would encourage me to go," she reasoned. "I have no future here. Surely life will be better in the United States."

Flora had tried for so long to please her mother, to change her mother's hate into love, but had failed on every try. "Maybe this way—sending the money she earned home—maybe . . ." She thought of the war. Staying in San Miguel would guarantee her a front-row seat—not a very pleasant thought.

Another possibility teased at her mind as she tossed about on her cot. Could she escape Carlotta's curse by leaving El Salvador? Flora decided she had good reasons to leave. Once she'd made her decision, sleep came.

Sunlight was flooding across Flora's cot when she awoke. Realizing she'd overslept, Flora bounded from bed, dressed, and hurried to help Ana prepare breakfast.

Flora wondered how she should approach the subject. She was forming the last breakfast tortilla when she announced, "Ana, I have decided to go and be with Aunt Carmelita—today!"

Ana frowned at her little sister. "You what?"

"I've decided to go to California." Flora picked up the platter of hot tortillas and carried them to the table.

Throughout the rest of the morning, no one mentioned Flora's decision. When Juan left the shop to deliver a packet of papers across town, Ana left also. Flora watched her sister disappear down the street. "Probably going to tell Mama," Flora thought.

She marveled at how good she felt. Instead of lamenting her fate, she found herself excited about the adventure. As Flora expected, Ana returned with Doña Alicia. Her mother and sister bade her follow them into the apartment. Flora obeyed. Her mother flipped the fringed shawl from her shoulders and turned to face her daughter. "What is this nonsense I hear about your going to the United States?"

"It's not nonsense, Mama," Flora defended. "I am leaving first thing in the morning."

"I don't believe you," her mother scoffed. "I won't believe it until I see you gone." Doña Alicia draped her shawl over the back of a dining-room chair.

"Believe what you wish," Flora replied, staring unflinchingly into her mother's hardened face. "I am going."

Beneath Flora's brave façade her courage had the consistency of jelly. She had never before stood up to her mother. She had never before stood up to anyone in her entire life, except the priest at the convent.

"Flora, this is such a serious step you're taking," Ana reminded. "You may never see your family again."

Flora glanced toward her sister. "I will never return to El Salvador until I can return with a doctor for my husband, and, and . . ." her words faltered, "and a Bible of my very own."

Flora wondered where she had gotten the idea about returning to El Salvador with a Bible and a doctor husband. The words just popped out somehow.

"Flora," Ana reminded, "it takes time to obtain the necessary papers that allow you to leave."

"Papa helped Marcos with the paperwork; he will help me also. I will take the bus to the capital to meet Papa tomorrow."

"I would go with you, if it weren't for my *niño*." Ana patted her stomach. "I'm afraid the bus ride would cause him to arrive too early."

Doña Alicia nodded. "You're right of course," she sighed. "I guess Rosa and I will have to go with her."

"I can manage by myself," Flora snapped, her lips pursed into a tight bow.

Doña Alicia's eyes snapped back with anger as she turned to her daughter. "Tsk! I will not have an unmarried daughter of mine traveling unattended," she snarled. "Once you leave the country, you may do as you wish; but while here, you will abide by our customs!" Doña Alicia paused to regain her self-control. "If you're really serious about leaving, you might as well gather your things and come home with me tonight so we can catch an early bus. I am sure your father's sister, Raquel, will house us until you leave the country."

Having declared her independence, Flora chafed at having to follow her mother's instructions. "Soon," she muttered to herself, "soon I shall be free. Yes, tomorrow will definitely be better."

Later that night, as she lay sleeping, Carlotta's apparition awakened Flora. The same chill settled in around her. The being spoke to her in a deep, raspy voice, not at all like Grandma Marta's. "Flora, you think you'll escape me in the United States." The room filled with a horrid laugh. "But I will be with you wherever you go. You will never be free of me. Never, never, never!" The apparition faded from view.

The chill lingered long after the being disappeared. Would she ever escape this fiend? Would she—could she ever be truly free? Flora wasn't sure.

She thought about her vow. "I think I understand why I said I wouldn't come back until I married a doctor. Dr. Diaz has been very kind. Besides, doctors are rich," she mumbled. "But a Bible? Why did I say I'd own a Bible before I returned?"

Chapter 8
Evening on the Town

The pre-World War II bus bounced along a rutted stretch of Pan American Highway outside of the capital city of San Salvador. While dust billowed through the open windows, passengers struggled to balance chickens, children, baskets, and bundles in the limited space. The passengers' once brightly colored clothing chosen especially for the great adventure to the capital now hung limp with sweat and grime.

Flora switched from one foot to the other. Loose strands of hair escaped her braid, circling her face with moist ringlets. A widening stain of perspiration laced the neckline of her pink cotton dress. She tightened her grip on the grimy, chrome-plated pole as the bus driver shifted gears to climb another hill.

An old man standing behind Flora jabbed his shopping basket into her spine. She grunted in pain. The wide-brimmed straw hat on the man sitting in front of her blocked the passing view. A woman struggled to keep a two-year-old boy from disappearing into the tangle of feet, baskets, and cages covering the floor.

The sound of people laughing and talking, mingled with squawking chickens and wailing babies, swirled around her. The discordant tunes from a lone harmonica player could be heard from somewhere farther back in the bus. It seemed like an unbelievable dream—or was it a nightmare? Flora wasn't sure.

"So this is the beginning of my big adventure," Flora thought. She refused to think about the airplane that would carry her to the United States. Often she had seen what seemed like tiny, silver birds soaring high above her village. And each time, she remembered the witch doctor's prediction that one day "this girl will fly."

As the bus jounced along the dusty jungle road, the driver swerved to miss a deep pothole in the road. Flora lurched forward, almost grabbing a young man's beard for support. Doña Alicia caught her arm in time. The man glared at them both. When the bus reached the Mercado Cuartel, San Salvador's shopping plaza, Flora breathed a sigh of relief.

She stepped off the bus into a profusion of color. Men and women dressed in reds, oranges, and yellows competed with the flower-laden basket stalls for attention. Amid real and paper blossoms, she stopped to admire the corn-husk flowers. Dipped in wax, the flowers looked so real one had to sniff them to be certain they were imitations.

Doña Alicia growled and hurried through the crowds, past the sisal bags and leather saddles, past the delicately crafted figurines, the brightly colored bedspreads, the hand-made wooden carvings and playful piñatas. Excited, Flora tried to absorb everything she saw.

After walking several blocks south from the marketplace, Doña Alicia paused before the winged monument to liberty in the Plaza Liberdad. While her mother and Rosa dutifully crossed themselves in front of El Rosario Cathedral, Flora craned her neck to admire the tiers of jewellike, stained-glass windows rising upward and inward from both sides of the church. Its beauty left her breathless. Reluctantly she allowed her mother and Rosa to lead her from the plaza.

Doña Alicia called for her to walk faster. She followed them into a massive stone building. When Flora stepped beneath the cool arches leading to her father's law offices, a wave of shyness overtook her. It had been years since she'd seen him. A vague image of him came to her mind.

Doña Alicia led the way down the hall and into a large office. She stopped at a massive oak desk and spoke to the carefully dressed secretary. After speaking into a small black box on her desk, the secretary motioned Doña Alicia into the inner office. Fifteen minutes later, the black box on the secretary's desk spoke. "Please send my daughter into my office," the box said.

As she stood, Flora glanced toward Rosa questioningly.

Rosa glanced up from the glossy magazine she'd been reading. "I will see him later." Flora stepped into the office.

Before her stood a tall, lean man, dressed in a white linen suit. He arose from his desk and introduced himself. "I am your father," he stated, pausing to size her up. "And you are

Floracita." A wide grin wreathed his face, "my little one."

She studied his face. "Yes," she thought, "my brother looks a lot like you. Ana's eyes are shaped like yours too."

"Your mother tells me you wish to go to the United States," he said, "and you want my help, is that it?"

"Yes sir," Flora answered hesitantly.

"Well," he stroked his small black goatee for a moment, "you know, there are many people trying to flee the country right now. It will not be easy. The army is already stopping vehicles heading north out of the city."

Her heart sank. "If I can't go to the United States, what will I do?" she thought. "I must go!" Determined, Flora lifted her chin, cleared her throat, and said, "I still wish to go."

"It could be dangerous." The man studied Flora's determined eyes for a moment, then shrugged. "I guess we'd better get the paperwork started. I will do all I can. I will arrange to have you stay with my sister, Raquel." With the wave of his hand, Marcos, the father, was transformed into Marcos le Fleur, Jr., attorney at law. "Now, if you will excuse me, I will make a phone call, after which I wish to speak with your mother for a moment."

Nerves gripped her stomach as she left her father's office. Rosa glanced up as Flora approached. "It's stuffy in here," Flora whispered. "I think I'll step out into the hall for a breath of fresh air." Rosa nodded and disappeared behind a glossy magazine.

As Flora restlessly paced up and down the main hall of her father's office building, a scruffy-looking young man leaned against the marble pillar watching.

"You are wishing to leave El Salvador, yes?" he whispered hurriedly into her ear as he suddenly fell into step beside her.

"I beg your pardon?"

"You are planning to leave El Salvador soon?"

"Who are you? How do you know that?" she asked, stopping long enough to size up the persistent young man. Besides needing a bath and a shave, his soiled army uniform spoke of hard wear and layers of sweat.

"These walls have ears." The man grasped her elbow and steered her out of the building onto the busy sidewalk. "Well, is it true? Are you leaving El Salvador?" he asked.

"Yes," she answered, tugging free from his grasp. "But what is that to you?"

"The army's closed the borders. They'll close the airport soon," he explained. "I have a truck and if you have a passport, I can smuggle you out of the country—for a small fee, of course."

Flora shielded her eyes from the sun and studied the stranger again. "When are you leaving?" she asked.

"Tomorrow evening, one hour after sundown."

Pondering her father's warnings, Flora wavered for a few seconds, then said, "No, I do not wish to go with you. My father will handle my travel arrangements. Thank you anyway."

During the next three days, Flora was shuffled back and forth from what seemed like every government office in the city until all the legal documents allowing her to leave El Salvador had been officially signed and stamped.

At her last stop, the American embassy, Flora took a deep breath as she entered the impressive stone building. She knew that if the embassy officials refused to stamp her visa, all her efforts had been in vain. She knew her chances were slim with so many Salvadorans requesting visas because of the threat of war with Honduras. After a three-hour wait, she entered a closetlike office. A sandy-haired young man, less than a decade beyond his teens, sat behind a cluttered mahogany desk.

"Why do you wish to go to the United States?" the young man asked, pushing his wire-rimmed glasses higher onto the bridge of his nose.

Her father had warned her not to mention that she might emigrate. "My aunt lives there," Flora answered, with all the confidence she could muster. "I am going to visit her."

"How long do you plan to stay?" he inquired, glancing up from the sheet of paper before him.

"Long enough to learn the English language."

The officer's watery blue eyes peered over the rims of his glasses. A slight sneer formed at the edges of his thin, colorless lips. "How can you, obviously a peasant, afford to make such a trip?"

"As you can see by my papers," she replied, elevating her nose a trifle for effect, "my father, Attorney Marcos le Fleur, Jr., is taking care of my travel expenses."

The officer's head jerked up at the mention of her father. A surprised "Oh!" escaped his lips. Flora smiled at the power of her father's name—even here, in the American Embassy. "Fine," he answered, shuffling the papers one more time and filling in various blanks as he went. Then without another word, he stamped each sheet with the official seal and handed them to Flora. "It looks like everything is in order. Have a nice trip."

From the moment Flora, Rosa, and Alicia arrived in El Salvador, the le Fleur relatives living in and around the city came to meet the three women and to tell Flora goodbye. Each evening they gathered around Aunt Raquel's stained oak dining table to eat and to give advice to the young adventuress.

"Ah, you must learn to dance," Aunt Elena suggested. "My Cecilia says that all the Americanos know how to dance. She's studying at Boston University, you know. Perhaps your cousin, Pablo, might take you dancing before you leave."

Another aunt shook her head and clucked her tongue. "Don't be offended, but your clothes are not acceptable. From what I see in the American fashion magazines, you will look out of place. I have a few things I don't wear any longer that may fit you."

Her married cousin, Maria, added, "And if you were staying longer, I could teach you how to make up your face like North American girls do."

Aunt Elena nodded her approval. Then her smile turned grave. "Flora is lucky to be getting out—escaping from the coming troubles. From what my brother, Marcos, tells me, it is only a matter of time until the Honduran army invades our borders, forcing our president to declare martial law. I wish my Pablo could go to the United States also."

"You would send him away?" The women gasped in horror.

"To save his life? Absolutely!"

Flora was relieved when the women switched to less frightening topics like the latest American movies and the newest recording artist from Argentina that made the hearts of all the woman of San Salvador beat faster.

On her last night in the capitol, Flora wished to escape the crowd at her Aunt Raquel's house, if only for a few hours. It was already dark when she mentioned to Aunt Elena that she'd hardly seen any of the Salvadoran capital. The woman, knowing the family would be scandalized if a young, single woman of Flora's age ventured out alone, volunteered her son to act as escort.

Such an act seemed a little silly to Flora since in the morning she would be flying all the way to Los Angeles by herself. But Pablo seemed as eager as she to escape confinement in the house. "Let's go to a disco," he suggested as soon as they'd left his parents' home.

"Disco?" Flora asked, "what is a disco?"

"You know! It's a place where you dance," he said, smirking at her ignorance. "You're a very pretty girl, you know, and you'll have no trouble picking up a date." Pablo led her across the busy street and down a side street toward the main part of town.

"A date?" she questioned.

"Yeah," he replied, "a date—you know, a man."

Flora gulped and shook her head resolutely. She had never before danced—let alone with a man. "No, I don't want to go. I do not know how to dance."

"Tomorrow you will be seventeen, right, and you've never had a date or danced? Well, now is a good time to learn," he insisted, taking Flora's arm and leading her down the street. "In the United States, everyone discos."

Flora stopped and jerked her arm from his grasp. "That may be so, but not me. As I said before, I wish to see the sights of the city."

Unaccustomed to having pretty girls, even cousins, refuse to do as he dictated, Pablo sneered, "Tour the city? Next you'll be telling me that you want to go to some, some church?" For emphasis, he pointed toward the small, white clapboard church near where they stood. A well-kept lawn with blossoming bougainvillea bushes surrounded the plain building.

The church's double doors stood ajar. Flora caught the sound of singing voices. Intrigued, she listened:

> Shall we gather at the river
> Where bright angel feet have trod,
> With its crystal tide forever
> Flowing by the throne of God?

Flora moved toward the church, as if drawn by a powerful magnet. Pablo reached out to stop her, but she continued walking until she reached the foot of the church steps.

Flora craned her neck and peered into the partially filled auditorium. Sensing a compelling warmth flowing toward her through the open doors, she fought to control a deluge of conflicting emotions.

"No!" she argued silently, "There is no room in my life for God or for religion!" And yet, the music beckoned her.

Suddenly she remembered Pablo's question. Half joking, she turned and announced, "That's not such a bad idea. I'd like to go in there."

"What?" Pablo gasped, horror suffusing his face. "You refuse to go with me to a disco, yet you would risk your eternal destiny by entering into a worship place of, of, of, heretics? I can't believe it!" Unable to restrain himself any longer, he grabbed her arm and pulled her back to the street. "You are a foolish girl, a very foolish girl. Promise me you will never leave the Holy Roman Catholic Church. Never, ever!"

"Don't worry," she sneered, "I am not interested in finding any new religions."

For the rest of the evening, Pablo took her to San Salvador's monuments and through its most impressive cathedrals, all the while exhorting her not to leave the mother church. "All other religions are heresy and abominations to God," he insisted.

"Yes, Pablo," Flora agreed, yet all the while the tune she'd heard outside the church played round and round in her head.

Both Flora and Pablo were exhausted and grateful that their evening on the town was over when they returned to the hacienda. Thankful that most of the family had already retired for the night, Flora breathed a sigh of relief and hurried to her room.

Once inside, Flora opened her old suitcase. Pushing aside the new dresses her aunt had given her, she lifted her jewelry box from its resting place. Carefully, she removed the rubber band and opened the lid.

She gazed at the contents of the box: snapshots of her family members, of herself when she was a little girl, a few pieces of cheap jewelry she'd been given over the years, and Señor Ortega's pages of Bible texts. She ran her fingers over the letters. A heavy sadness filled her mind. Returning her treasures to the box, she yawned and slipped the rubber band into place "I guess there's no turning back now," she thought. "Come morning, I really am leaving."

Chapter 9
Escape in the Night

Flora squeezed her eyes shut, blocking out the blur of government buildings speeding by on the narrow, predawn street. Her eyes flew open in terror as the taxi careened around another sharp corner. "Why am I doing this?" she screamed silently. She dared not look toward her sister, Rosa, or Mama. She feared once her tears began falling, they might never stop. "No matter what happens, I won't cry. *I won't!*"

Her hands clutched the camel-brown leather purse Aunt Raquel had given her. She thought of the U.S. currency inside it. It was the first pocketbook and the first money she'd ever owned. Although the bills looked strange compared to the Salvadoran colons, her father assured her they were very real and that she must guard them carefully. She could feel the hard sides of the English-to-Spanish dictionary inside the purse also. Her father had called the book her lifeline to survival.

Outside the dusty window, the parade of government buildings gave way to empty shops and darkened homes. It was difficult to believe while the unsuspecting San Salvadorans slept, government soldiers were gathering at the city limits, to enforce martial law on the city and the entire country.

Less than an hour before, she'd been sleeping peacefully in her bed when her Aunt Raquel shook her awake.

"Flora! Flora, wake up," her aunt called. "You must wake up if you plan to leave the country. Hurry!"

"Huh?" the sleepy girl moaned. "What time is it? Is it morning?" She stretched and yawned.

"It's a little after three." Aunt Raquel pulled the girl to a sitting position. "Come on! Your mother and Rosa are already dressing. You must leave for the airport now!"

"But my plane doesn't leave until nine," Flora mumbled, longing to return to the comfort of sleep.

"Flora!" Aunt Raquel dragged the girl's legs over the side of the bed. "Wake up! Your father has sent word that Honduran soldiers have invaded our country from the east and the north," Aunt Raquel explained in agitation. "Martial law will be declared within the hour. All highways will be blocked; all trains and airlines will be brought to a halt—indefinitely!"

Aunt Raquel urged Flora to her feet. "The last plane leaves in forty-five minutes. Your father has phoned in your reservations. If you want to go to California, you'd better move now."

The entire household scurried about helping the women prepare to leave for the airport. Minutes later, a taxi stopped at the front gate. While Flora, Rosa, and Doña Alicia raced to the car, the taxi driver grabbed Flora's suitcase and tossed it into the trunk.

Stepping quickly into the cab, Flora took one last look out the back window of the cab at her new-found relatives huddled around the front gate to see her off. Meanwhile the driver slammed the cab door shut and climbed into the front seat.

Doña Alicia leaned forward and tapped the man on the shoulder. "Please hurry," she urged, "my daughter's flight for Mexico City is leaving minutes from now." The taxi leaped forward as the cabbie stepped on the accelerator.

Flora grabbed for the armrest as the vehicle raced down the darkened streets of the city.

Taking a deep breath, Flora leaned back against the tattered upholstery and glanced toward her mother. "I'll miss you, Mama," she mouthed, unable to break the pervading silence within the cab. "In spite of everything, I will miss you. Will you miss me too?"

Doña Alicia stared straight ahead, apparently unaware of her daughter's inner anguish. To Flora, her mother's eyes seemed normal—blank, cold, void of compassion. Through the years, she'd seen her vitality fade into zombielike disinterest.

A vision of the hated Carlotta flashed through Flora's mind. She could hear the woman's high-pitched, crackly voice. "You will one day fly like a bird up in the sky." Feeling like a five-year-old again, Flora shuddered.

Again the witch's raspy voice cackled within Flora's brain, "You think you can escape me—going to this new country, but you can't. My curse will follow you always." Flora glanced at her mother, at Rosa, and at the cab driver. Could they hear Carlotta's threat? "No, no," she realized.

"I will escape," she argued. " I will escape from you, from Arturo, from Juan, from my mother. I will be free—totally free."

Without warning, the cabbie braked, propelling the three women hard against the front seat. Leaping from the vehicle, he threw open the car door. "We're here, Señorita—at the airport," he announced, grinning proudly, "and on time! I will get your suitcase."

Flora stepped from the car and turned toward the small Quonset building that served as an air terminal. While her mother paid the driver, a nameless terror seized Flora. She walked through the airport and onto the airfield like a wind-up toy. She neither saw nor responded to the flight personnel hurrying her toward the plane. The twenty-year-old vintage "bird" seemed monstrous to the frightened young woman. She wondered if such a gigantic creature could get off the ground. At the foot of the steps, she turned toward her sister.

"Goodbye," Rosa wept, kissing Flora on the cheek. "Come back to us someday."

"When I have a Bible and a doctor-husband," Flora sniffed, tears welling up in her eyes. She reached for her mother, but the woman only stared, stone-faced at Flora's outstretched arms. Momentarily, their eyes met. Then, without a word, Doña Alicia turned and walked back toward the terminal. Rosa threw a quick, pitying look at her sister and ran after Doña Alicia.

Flora gasped, overwhelmed by her mother's evident rejection. A hand grabbed her and dragged her into the plane. "We've got to leave now!" A man shouted. As she stepped on board, she felt the quaking craft inch forward. "Please, miss," the man insisted, "take your seat immediately."

Flora was certain the plane would shake to pieces before it ever got airborne. She stumbled to the only empty seat left and sat down. "This is it," she thought, her stomach quivering like green coconut jelly. "No turning back now."

Like it or not, she would go to the United States or die trying. She looked around at the plane's shabby interior. "Whether I die in this coffin or in far-off California makes little difference," she thought to herself.

ESCAPE IN THE NIGHT 51

Suddenly a passenger shouted and pointed toward the end of the landing strip. "Look! Army trucks!"

The passengers strained to get a better view of the long column of military vehicles racing toward the moving airplane. A sense of growing panic pervaded the cabin. As the jeeps drew closer, the airplane continued gaining speed. It looked as if the vehicles would collide before the plane could become airborne. "Then again," her thoughts resumed, "maybe the only place I'll go is to prison."

Loud cheers erupted from the passengers when the plane lifted off the ground. The passengers, mostly businessmen, laughed and gesticulated obscenely at the uniformed officer standing in his jeep, waving frantically for the pilot to stop.

As the aircraft circled high in the sky, the passengers relaxed—some to sleep and others to study papers from the fine leather briefcases on their laps.

Flora's face remained frozen to the window. The sight of the land dropping dramatically away from her, and not the soldiers, were her main concern. The craft climbed high over the jungle and angled toward the horizon.

A gentle tap on her wrist startled her. She turned toward the mustachioed businessman across the aisle from her. "You'd better put your seatbelt on," he suggested. "It will probably be a bumpy ride."

"Seatbelt?" she asked. "What is a seatbelt?"

The man smiled and pointed at the nylon straps lying on each side of her lap. He showed her how to fasten the belt. She smiled and whispered a thank you, then returned her attention to the window. She watched as the sun climbed high into the sky. Every now and then, she could spot a clearing in the forest canopy—revealing a village or a plantation. Before long, there were more clearings and less jungle until the landscape gave way to hundreds of buildings of every size.

"That's Mexico City," the businessman explained.

As the plane circled for a landing, Flora strained to watch miniature cars and trucks scoot along the narrow ribbons of asphalt branching out in every direction. She could hardly believe that full-sized people were riding in those tiny machines.

When the concrete runway rose to meet their plane, Flora gasped and her knuckles whitened from the death grip she had on the seat's armrests. She exhaled only after the plane's wheels touched the ground. By the time she figured out how to unfasten the seatbelt, the plane had come to a stop beside the massive steel-and-glass terminal.

Following the other passengers down the metal stairs, Flora stared in fascination at the gigantic aircraft on each side of the plane she had ridden. The propeller-driven plane she had imagined to be so big back in San Salvador was dwarfed next to these monstrosities.

Entering the main terminal, she glanced about, uncertain as to what she should do next. All around her, people rushed by. To Flora, it seemed as if the entire population of Mexico City, and possibly all of Mexico, had come to the airport that day. She had never seen so many people in her entire life—even during her short tour of San Salvador. And they all acted like they were going to a celebration.

She had only walked twenty or thirty feet along the main concourse when a dark-complexioned man dressed in a business suit sidled up to her. "Excuse me, I am looking for a woman friend. Could it possibly be you?" he smiled engagingly, revealing a wide expanse of white teeth beneath a bushy mustache.

"I-I-I don't think so," Flora stammered, stepping to one side in order to pass.

"Your name is . . . ?" he inquired, slipping his arm about her shoulders.

"I am Flora le Fleur," answered Flora, edging away from the stranger. "My father is sending me to the United States."

The man's mustached grin grew even wider. "Yes, that's right. I knew you were the girl I was looking for, Flora. Your father, Señor le Fleur asked me to watch over you while you were here in Mexico city," he assured her as he maneuvered her through the crowds.

"You say you know my father, Señor?"

The man threw his head back and laughed. "Call me Julio. Your Father and I do business together often. Whenever he flies to Mexico City, he stays at my home."

"Excuse, Señor," Flora began, "but where are we going? I am really very hungry. I had to leave El Salvador rather quickly this morning."

"Ah, you wish to eat?" His eyes brightened. "First, we will go to a bar for a little drink, then I will take you to my apartment for a fine meal."

"Go with you?" Flora shook her head. "I will miss my flight to California."

"No, no, no. My apartment isn't far from here. I have a car waiting outside. We have plenty of time," the man continued talking nonstop as he ushered Flora through the crowded airport. "You will like my little place."

Flora sensed that something was wrong. She looked about nervously for a way to escape. Just having the man's arm on her shoulder made her shudder. Suspicious that Julio was up to no good, Flora was resolved not to leave the airport with him. Suddenly a familiar sign up ahead gave her an idea.

"Please, Señor . . ."

"Julio, call me Julio."

"Please Julio, I need to use the ladies' rest room," she pointed to the sign.

A frown darkened the man's face. But he replaced it quickly with another toothy smile. "Certainly, my dear. I will wait right here for you."

"Fine." Flora disappeared into the ladies' room. "Ah," she thought, staring at herself in the mirror, "another Arturo or Juan. Perhaps my Unseen Power is still with me, even in Mexico City."

Flora made herself comfortable on an orange vinyl lounge. Her stomach growled as she watched well-dressed ladies touch up their makeup and adjust their hairdos before the wall of mirrors. "All right, Unseen Power, You helped me escape; now make Julio go away so I won't miss my plane. And, by the way," she added, "I am still very hungry."

After a while Flora eyed an elegantly dressed matron primping before the mirror. The woman smiled. Taking a deep breath of courage, Flora stepped up to her and asked if a man in a tan business suit was waiting outside.

The woman peered out of the doorway this way and that and shook her head. "No Señorita, no one is out there."

"Good," Flora replied.

Fifteen minutes later, Flora ventured out onto the concourse, scanning the faces in the crowd as she went. Satisfied Julio had given up, Flora set out to find her departure gate.

Chapter 10
Uniformed Terror

A surge of exhilaration mixed with trepidation flowed through Flora as the plane landed at Los Angeles International Airport. She patted her leather purse gently, assuring herself it still contained her Spanish-to-English dictionary.

After announcing the arrival instructions in both English and Spanish, the head stewardess added, "After you deboard, please proceed directly to customs."

The waiting area was clean, new-smelling, sterile—and cold. Outside the walls of glass, hundreds of vehicles and street lights glowed, turning the night into day. Tears swam before her eyes as she stared at the confusing, unfamiliar world awaiting her.

The day had been an exhausting, stomach-wrenching series of reverberating airports, muffled announcements, most of which Flora couldn't understand, a barrage of strange foods and drinks, and solicitous, efficient attention by plane employees. Flora found it hard to believe that such opulence could exist.

Fear like a school of hungry piranhas gnawed at Flora's stomach as she retrieved her luggage and joined the long line of passengers going through customs. She shook uncontrollably as the line shortened. Her inbred fear of any sort of uniformed official became almost impossible to control. "I mustn't panic. I mustn't panic," she thought, reminding herself how father had assured her every one of her papers was meticulously in order.

When she reached the head of the line, her terror intensified at the sight of the sober-faced, customs official. The middle-aged man studied her papers carefully. Barely looking up, he spoke with machine-gun speed, "Where did you get this visa?"

Flora's dark eyes widened at his angry tone. "I don't speak English," she explained, reaching for her open purse lying on the narrow formica-covered table. "My dictionary," she thought, "I need my dictionary."

His hand clamped down on top of hers as he repeated his question in Spanish.

"From the embassy in San Salvador," Flora replied in short gasps.

"Hmph! I doubt that! Follow me, please!" He scooped up her belongings and led the way down a narrow hallway to a cubicle of an office. He opened the door and indicated she should enter. "You are in serious trouble. You may have to spend the night in jail. At best, you'll be shipped back to El Salvador," he added, tossing her things on the cluttered desktop. "Sit down and stay put until I return with my supervisor," he ordered.

Two hours later, the official returned and reluctantly allowed Flora to leave the office with a last warning as he let her go. "If your documents are forged, you will be caught and deported, you know. I will personally see to it!"

Outside the airport's main entrance, the cool night air nipped at Flora's bare arms. Accustomed to balmy tropical evenings, the mid-December temperatures of southern California penetrated Flora's thin cotton peasant blouse, chilling her to the bone. She rubbed her arms briskly and paced back and forth in front of the electronic doors.

For a time, Flora hovered inches beyond the large plate-glass windows separating the terminal from the arriving automobile traffic. She peered about, certain a customs agent lurked nearby, waiting for her to commit some heinous crime so he could send her back to El Salvador. Slowly she became aware of a uniformed black man watching her from farther down the sidewalk.

In El Salvador, the only blacks she'd ever seen were the laborers imported from Honduras to pick the coffee crops. Flora had never seen a uniformed black man, and to her, a uniform implied authority, and authority implied—disaster.

To quell her paranoia, she watched the various colored lights. Whenever a patrol car approached or a uniformed security guard strode past, she shrank into the shadows.

Restless, she peered through the plate-glass windows at the clock on the wall behind the closest ticket counter—9:00 p.m. She had been waiting an hour and a half.

"I wonder where Aunt Carmelita can be," she thought, glancing nervously toward the black man. "There he is, staring again. I wish he would go away," she thought.

Flora reread her aunt's letter. "Could Aunt Carmelita have forgotten me? Did she not get the message of my arrival? No, there's no mistake," she thought. Except for the seven numbers at the end of the letter, everything was in order. After stuffing the letter back into her purse, she began pacing again.

Nine-thirty, ten, ten-thirty, eleven. Cars came and left. Feeling cold and abandoned, Flora studied each face, hoping to recognize her aunt. She thought about the few articles of clothing in her suitcase and realized none would be warm enough to ward off the cold. Her stomach growled from hunger.

Suddenly, a heavy bass voice behind her spoke. She jumped and whirled about in surprise. "Pardon me, miss," he said in English, "may I help you? Do you need to call someone?"

She lifted her eyes to the black face towering more than a foot above her five-foot-one inch stature. "No comprendo Inglez," she answered, all the while inching toward the automatic doors.

"You look mighty cold. Here, take my jacket for a few minutes." The black man offered her his red jacket.

"No! No!" she shook her head frantically.

"But you are cold," he insisted.

"No!"

The porter studied her face for a moment, then shrugged. An automobile had pulled up in front of his station. He hurried toward the curb to help the incoming passengers with their luggage. Flora sighed with relief.

The temperature continued to drop until by midnight, her teeth chattered uncontrollably. Repeatedly, the porter attempted to communicate with her. As she flipped through her dictionary to decipher his message, Flora decided that the first thing she had to do was to learn English. Little by little, Flora began to understand that the man was trying to help. Shyly, she removed her aunt's letter from the purse and handed it to him.

"I don't speak Spanish," he admitted, scanning the letter, "and those who do have long since gone home for the night—hey, wait a minute!" He pointed to the numbers at the end of the letter. "A telephone number. Did you try to call this number? I'll bet they're waiting for your call right now."

Again Flora shook her head. "No English."

UNIFORMED TERROR 57

Without another word, the man grabbed her suitcase with one hand, her elbow with the other, and steered her into the terminal. Frightened, she struggled to break free, but the man held on too tightly.

He guided her to one of the pillars in the waiting area. "Here," he said, "a phone. Call your friends."

Again Flora shook her head; her large brown eyes filled with confusion. "N-n-no comprendo," she stammered.

He picked up the receiver and thrust it into her hand. She stared first at the black object, then back at the man.

After a moment, he scratched his head in amazement. "Haven't you ever seen a telephone?" He stopped. "That's it, isn't it?" The porter laughed and took the receiver from her hands.

After a few seconds of fiddling with the other end of the strange-looking object, he dropped a handful of coins into it. Then he held the black object to his ear and spoke into it.

After a few moments he handed the black object to Flora. The sound of a human voice speaking to her from the machine startled her and caused her to drop the receiver. But even as it dangled from its spiral cord, she could still hear someone speaking to her. She picked up the receiver and held it to her ear.

"Flora? Flora? Is that you?" a voice called. "Hola? Hola?"

"Hola?" she answered timidly.

"This is your aunt. Why didn't you call me earlier? That man said you've been waiting at the airport since 7:30 this evening."

"Call you? I did not know how to."

"Oh my goodness!" her aunt exclaimed, suddenly switching from Spanish to English. "She's never used a telephone before."

"I do not . . ."

"It's OK," her aunt assured her. "I will come and get you right away. Just stay put. I'll be there in two hours."

Flora nodded in agreement.

"Do you understand?" her aunt questioned again.

"Huh?" Oh yes. I will stay right here," Flora replied.

After her aunt said goodbye, Flora handed the receiver to the porter and said, "Gracias, señor."

The porter grinned, "That I understand—glad I could help."

Chapter 11
A Place of Her Own

Flora followed Carmelita up the walk to a small stucco house, pausing as her aunt unlocked the door and stepped inside.

"Well, come on in," Carmelita invited, tossing her suitcase case onto the soiled, olive-green sofa. "My roommates are at work. Mr. Ricardo, our landlord lives in the big house. He doesn't know you are here yet."

Crossing to the kitchen counter, Carmelita twisted a dial on a small brown box. Flora eyed it suspiciously as a man's voice filled the room. This was quickly followed by music, or at least Flora thought it was music.

Carmelita laughed at her niece's reaction. "This is a radio. See, you turn this knob to make it louder or softer. This other knob is for changing stations. Go ahead and put your stuff in the bedroom."

Flora walked through the living room and the kitchen into the bedroom. Except for a crucifix and some magazine pictures, the walls were bare. Four beds, each with a different colored chenille spread, were lined up military style against one wall. Along the opposite wall was a bureau.

"You can use the second bed from the window," Carmelita said.

"We all sleep in the same room, my two roommates and me, and now you," her aunt explained, opening one of the drawers in the six-drawer dresser for Flora's inspection. "I've cleared out this drawer for you. Your other clothes can hang in the hall closet."

While her aunt made a trip to a nearby convenience market, Flora unpacked her suitcase. Carmelita returned after a few minutes with a quart of milk and a loaf of white bread. Then she removed a suitcase from the closet and tossed it onto one of the beds.

Flora watched silently as Carmelita packed the case. "Why are you packing? Are you going away?"

"For the weekend. I hope you don't mind. My roommates and I have been planning this trip to Las Vegas for some time now. I'm meeting them downtown in an hour, so I have to hurry," Carmelita explained. "Of course, I suppose you could come along..."

The tone in Carmelita's voice caused Flora to tense and hesitate. "No, no, I will be all right."

"Good!" Carmelita leaned toward the oval mirror over the dresser, puckered her lips, and applied a fresh coat of ruby-red lipstick. After patting her short dark curls, she sprayed them with hairspray and turned to her bewildered niece. "It is important that you not be seen," she cautioned. "Do not go out of the apartment or even look out a window until I return—and no lights on at night. Señor Ricardo will throw us out onto the street if he finds out you are here."

Flora lingered in the living-room doorway while her aunt rushed through the apartment packing last-minute items. "There's food in the cupboards and the refrigerator," Carmelita informed her. "Remember, don't let anyone know you're here." Then her aunt was gone.

With nothing to do and nowhere to go, Flora slipped off her sandals and padded through the empty apartment. By midafternoon the drawn curtains and closed blinds caused a melancholy darkness to fill the apartment. Flora sighed. Her stomach growled. She was hungry again.

She studied the refrigerator. She'd watched her aunt open the door to put the milk away. Carefully, Flora opened the door and peered inside. All the shelves were empty except for the milk carton sitting on the top shelf. Flora glanced at the cupboards. All she found was the loaf of bread her aunt had purchased.

"I'd better wait until later to eat," she thought as she strolled into the living room and stretched out on the sofa. "If I'm careful, the food should last until Monday." A stack of fashion magazines lying on the floor beside the sofa caught her attention. She picked up the top magazine and leafed through it. She paused to study the photo of a model with flowing, platinum-blond hair.

The woman was wearing a white diaphanous negligee.

"If this is what it takes to be an American," she decided, "I'll never make it." She dropped the magazine on the floor and closed her eyes.

Visions of cool jungle undergrowth replaced the faded wallpaper in her aunt's living room. The blond model's lovely face melted like wax into the face of Flora's cherished picture of the bride doll. Then slowly, the doll's features darkened, her hair seemed to catch the shadows of the jungle, becoming a deep, chocolate brown. As the doll ran along the narrow pathway, Flora heard her own voice, "I'm hungry, Please Mama, I am so hungry."

Suddenly the skirt of her white satin gown caught on briars. She pulled it free only to discover rips and tears from the thorns. She ran on until she tripped over a vine and fell in a giant mud puddle. As the doll got back up on her feet and turned around, Flora recognized the doll as herself.

A familiar cackle filled the jungle—Carlotta. "You will never escape, Flora. Never!"

Flora awoke with a start and found herself shivering with fright. She grasped her throat to still her accelerated breathing and wiped cold sweat from her forehead.

She glanced about the messy room. "I need to do something—anything!" she said. She hurried to the kitchen in search of a broom and dustpan.

The wail of a distant police siren caused her to freeze in her tracks. Curfew! Invasion! She ran into the bedroom and crawled beneath her aunt's bed. Flora waited for the sound of jeeps entering the neighborhood and a familiar voice shouting over the bullhorn. When none came, she crawled out from under the bed and peeked out the window.

On the lawn between her aunt's house and the landlord's, an old man stood hosing the flowers. As Flora watched, a white-haired woman folded a lawnchair and placed it in the shed beside the house. When the woman glanced toward Flora, she dropped the curtain, praying she hadn't been seen.

By now, her occasional hunger pang had become a gnawing ache. Carefully Flora poured a small portion of milk into a jelly glass and removed a slice of bread from the loaf.

Night fell. Shadows filled the rooms. Flora soon decided the only thing left for her to do was to go to bed. Except for a leaky faucet dripping in the bathroom, all was silent. For some time she lay awake listening to the unfamiliar noises seeping in from outside.

Monday came and went. Carmelita didn't return. Flora began to worry. Perhaps there had been an accident. Perhaps her aunt was hurt—or worse! Each evening, after dark, she would peek out of the curtains.

She drank the last half glass of milk on Tuesday evening. Her experience with famines and unexpected military invasions warned her that conditions could get worse so, she cut her rations in half.

A week passed. No one came near the apartment. When tempted to peek out the windows during the daylight hours, Flora remembered the customs agent's threats of sending her back to El Salvador. And each night, her "grandmother's spirit" visited her.

The second Monday and Tuesday dragged by. Hunger gnawed at her continually. On Wednesday, she broke her last two slices of bread into four small squares. If Carmelita didn't return soon, Flora realized she'd have to disobey her aunt and search for food.

On Thursday night, Flora gave in to despair. "Did I come so far to end up dying like this?" She fell into a heap beside the sofa. "Where is that Power when I need it?" She cried until she had no more tears, too exhausted to complain any longer. She hadn't been asleep long when the front door burst open.

Bolting awake, Flora jumped to her feet, her eyes widened with fear. A strange man silhouetted the doorway. Trembling beyond control, she opened her mouth to scream, but no sound came out.

The man stared dumbfounded at the young woman. In a flurry of Spanish, he asked, "What are you doing here? I didn't know you'd returned from Nevada?"

"I-I-I-b-b-but I never went," Flora stammered, backing into a footstool. Her knees buckled beneath her. She landed with a resounding thump on the stool.

"My mother-in-law was right," he said. "She said she saw someone at the window. I didn't believe her. Have you been in here long?"

Flora nodded.

"I came to fix the leaky faucet you girls have been complaining about." The man peered down at Flora and scratched his head. "But you're not one of the girls that rent from me," he added. "I've never seen you before."

Flora stared up in the man's rough, unshaven face, certain he would beat her, then throw her into jail. "N-n-n-o," she said, her voice catching in her throat like stitches on a basted hem. "I am Carmelita's niece f-f-f-from El Salvador."

"El Salvador? My wife and I are from El Salvador. When did you get here?" The landlord bombarded her with questions. "Have you eaten recently?"

Flora shook her head slowly.

His brow wrinkled. "Come over to my place. My wife, Francisca, will enjoy fattening you up. How about some scrambled eggs?"

Flora didn't have to be invited twice. Then she remembered. "B-b-but I have no money to pay you for food."

The man waved her objection aside. "You will repay us by serenading grandma and grandpa with stories of home—El Salvador."

Mr. Ricardo was right. Flora was welcomed into his family with open arms. As she ravenously devoured the scrambled eggs and beans on the homemade tortillas, she was certain nothing had ever tasted so good. Between mouthfuls, she answered questions about her war-torn country and about her trip to the States. The Ricardos ate the news of their country with as much enthusiasm as she ate the eggs, beans, and tortillas.

"Have you found a job yet?" Mrs. Ricardo asked as she filled Flora's plate a third time.

"A job? Do I have to work?"

Mr. Ricardo threw his head back and laughed. "Oh yes," he answered. "Everybody works here in America."

Flora blanched. "But I don't speak the language. How can I get a job?"

Mr. Ricardo studied the girl for a few moments. "If you wish, I'll take you to a place where my niece works. Maybe you can work there as a maid."

Flora nodded enthusiastically.

Before long Flora was working for a wealthy Jewish couple.

But instead of being hired as a maid she worked as a nursemaid for their newborn daughter, Hillary. Through sign language, the mistress of the home explained that Flora was to do no housework, no cooking, only care for the baby. She would have most evenings and one day off a week and be paid $25 a week, plus room and board.

The mistress led Flora to a one-room guest house behind the main mansion. White ruffled curtains edged a large picture window overlooking the family pool and sun deck. "This is your home," the woman explained. "You may do as you wish in here."

Once alone in the room, Flora whirled about, her dark eyes sparkling with happiness. A home, a real home of her own? A place where she really belonged?

Flora admired the splashy yellow-and-orange print wallpaper. Taking off her shoes, she bounced once or twice on the twin bed. She counted the drawers in the oak dresser "four, five, six! All mine?" she exclaimed. "I can't believe it." She never imagined she'd live in such luxury. Flora caught her own reflection in the large mirror over the bureau "You are very, very lucky!" she told her reflection.

After trying out the easy chair and turning the reading lamp on the small stand on and off a number of times, she inspected her bathroom. She ran her hand across the cool white tiles and caressed the fluffy bath towels. When the pleasure she felt inside spilled out, she hugged herself and laughed aloud. "Maybe my tomorrow has finally arrived," she whispered, afraid Carlotta's spirits might be hovering close by, waiting to ruin her happiness.

Chapter 12
A Stranger in Israel

The creaks from the overstuffed rocker accompanied Flora as she hummed softly to the infant sleeping on her lap. She leaned back against the chair and sighed. It seemed like forever since she left home. Each week she sent the major portion of her paycheck to her mother as promised. Though Flora included a letter with each paycheck, she seldom received one in return.

Her employers being Jewish, did not celebrate Christmas. As the holiday season approached, Flora missed the traditional decorations from her country. She remembered the luminaries (votive candles inside small bags of sand) lining the walkway to every door in the village. "Even if I don't believe the stories any longer, I miss it."

On Christmas Eve, she decided to attend Christmas mass at the large cathedral near the Foss's home. But the magnificent building lacked the warmth she remembered experiencing as a child. The worshipers and the rituals felt as foreign to her as every other aspect of her life in the United States. She plodded homeward after the service knowing she'd not return to church any time soon.

In the meantime, the Foss's preparations for the Hanukkah festivities filled Flora's days, especially after the arrival of Hillary's great grandmother. Flora enjoyed the old woman's company, even if she could speak only Spanish and Grandma could speak only Yiddish. "Hanukkah, the Festival of Dedication, is a 2,000-year-old festival that celebrates the Jewish refusal to assimilate into the majority culture," Grandma struggled to explain. Thankful for the adult company, Flora nodded agreement and smiled.

The woman continued to describe each custom in broken English, from the eight days of candle lighting to the specially prepared food and celebration. Flora enjoyed hearing Grandma sing the songs of Hanukkah. Their friendship grew with each of Grandma's monthly visits. When Grandma Foss became ill and moved into the home, Flora cheerfully accepted the responsibility of caring for her.

"She's so like Grandma Marta," Flora mused, "—the real one, not Carlotta's creation."

Grandma grew stronger each day. Before long, she joined Flora on her daily walks with Hillary. Each Friday, Grandma instructed Flora on the keeping of the Sabbath. "Shabbat means to cease or stop," the woman explained. "It is a day the family members rest from their labor. There is much preparation for Shabbat. We must make the *Challah* together."

Side by side the two women formed the round loaves of Sabbath bread. "It is the custom to tear off one piece of the unbaked *challah*, bless it, and burn it." While the *challah* baked, Grandma set the family table. A large pot of soup served as the main food during the Sabbath hours. "You see," she explained, "Jehovah gave us this day as a special sign between Him and us."

Though Flora was never allowed to join in on these special occasions, the ceremony fascinated her. She couldn't understand Grandma's definition of the Sabbath as a day when no one worked. From her perspective, it was the busiest day of the week.

During the months she'd been caring for Hillary and Grandma, Flora felt she'd been gently wrapped in a warm blanket of security. Her days had never been happier. But each night, her fears returned.

"Will you never go away?" the girl asked Carlotta's spirit one night.

"Only when you submit yourself to me."

"But Carlotta is more than a thousand miles away now," Flora replied.

"I do not need Carlotta. But I do need you." The more insistent the being became, the more Flora resisted. Yet, each night, as she anticipated the spirit's arrival, she trembled with fear. And, come morning, her fears receded into the shadows.

Flora longed to understand English. When Regina, a Mexican girl who worked in the house across the boulevard from the Foss estate, said she studied English two evenings a week at one of the local schools, Flora determined to do the same.

She had two choices. She could either attend the convent school in Hollywood or the public school across town in Glendale. For Flora, the choice was simple. She'd long since decided there was no room in her life for God. When she approached Mrs. Foss with her plan, the woman wasn't too pleased. She knew that if Flora learned English, she would be able to find a better-paying job. "It is a long way to Glendale," Mrs. Foss explained. "I will agree to take you there. But to return home, you are on your own. You will have to change buses twice and walk the last half mile up the hill from the bus stop."

Flora was so excited about going back to school, even the walk in the dark didn't stop her. Mrs. Foss kept her word and drove Flora to the Glendale school at 6:25 the following Monday evening. After filling out the necessary registration papers with the help of a friendly translator, Flora inched her way down the hall to Mr. Carter's class—room 191. The class was already in progress. Trying to be as inconspicuous as possible, Flora slipped into the first available seat. A tall, willowy girl, with the wide, almond-shaped eyes sat in the seat next to her.

"Hola," the girl whispered, "My name's Alejandra. Mr. Carter is taking roll."

"Hola," Flora replied. "You speak Spanish?"

"Of course. I'm from Mexico," Alejandra replied. "Where are you from?"

"El Salvador."

From the front of the classroom, a deep bass voice interrupted, "If you girls must talk, please do it in English."

The girls reddened and turned toward the instructor. "It's all right," he reassured them, "I was just teasing. But now that I have everyone's attention, we shall introduce ourselves—in English."

The class was like none Flora had ever attended. Mr. Carter, a man who volunteered his time to teach English to immigrants, kept the atmosphere relaxed and friendly. The students were of all ages and from places as varied as Columbia, Guatemala, Honduras, Panama, and Mexico. Just being with people who spoke and understood Spanish eased Flora's loneliness.

The two girls sitting near Flora introduced themselves. "My

name is Maria," whispered the first girl. Then turning to the other, said, "This is Noemi. We're just visiting."

Mr. Carter welcomed the students, then began his evening's instruction.

Each week the two visiting girls attended the classes, always sitting in the seats right behind Flora with the girl named Alejandra. One Wednesday, Flora was disappointed to discover Alejandra was absent. She joined Maria and Noemi. During the class break, the girls offered to buy Flora a soda. As they stood in the hall sipping their sodas, Maria asked, "How long have you been in the United States?"

Flora thought for a moment. "About a year," she replied.

"Do you live around here?" Noemi queried.

"No, I work for a family in Hollywood. My employer brings me to the school, and I ride the bus home," she explained.

Maria wrinkled her brow. "That's a long way from here. Would you like to ride home with us tonight?"

"Yeah," Noemi interjected, "we have plenty of time before we go home."

"You have a car?" Flora stared incredulously.

"Of course," Maria replied.

"It would be nice," Flora answered timidly, "if it's not out of your way."

Maria laughed and patted Flora's arm. "No problem. Glad to do it."

"I thought you were born in this country," Noemi added. "You don't have the heavy accent some immigrants have."

"Thank you." Flora beamed with delight since class was the only place she dared use her newly acquired language.

At the end of class, Flora followed her new friends to the parking lot and climbed into the back seat of a battered green Mustang. Noemi climbed into the passenger side of the car as Maria slid behind the wheel.

"Do you get any other time off during the week besides Wednesday?" Noemi asked.

Flora leaned forward, her elbows resting on the back of the seat. "Oh yes, sometimes I get Saturday off; at other times I get Sunday."

"Oh really?" Maria interrupted. "Would you like to go to church with us sometime?"

"I would, but this weekend I'm off on Saturday," Flora replied.

"That's OK. That's when we attend church," Maria chirped, "on Saturday."

"Are, are you Jews?" Flora asked, confused as to how such a thing might be possible.

"Oh, no," Noemi answered. "We are Christian, just like you." Suddenly Flora froze. Then her mind flashed back to Mother Superior at the convent school and Señor Ortega, her Saturday-keeping teacher.

When Flora didn't reply, Maria peered at her through the rear-view mirror. "We'd love to take you."

"I don't know," Flora floundered, searching for a reasonable alibi. On one hand, she'd vowed to stay away from churches and God. On the other, she was curious about a church where they worshiped on the same day as Señor Ortega worshiped. "What do you do in your church?"

Now it was Maria's turn to pause. "Well, we sing songs and we study the Bible."

A electric shock shook Flora's body. "The Bible? You don't mean you study the Bible. You mean that your priest reads from the Bible and you listen, don't you?"

The two girls in the front seat looked at one another and laughed. "No," Noemi explained. "Each person brings his own Bible, and we study together.

"And in Spanish too," Maria added.

"That sounds too good to be true," Flora responded skeptically. "You mean everyone brings Bibles? I can't believe that."

"Honestly, we do," Noemi reassured her. "And I'll even prove it to you. I'll give you one next Sabbath morning."

"You would give me a Bible printed in Spanish?" Flora eyed her friend, questioningly. "You would not joke about something so important to me, would you?"

"No, of course not," Maria answered seriously. "But why is it so hard for you to believe?" Glancing at Flora's serious expression, she added, "Would you believe me if I got one for you right now?"

"Do you really mean that? Would you?" Flora asked with rising excitement.

"Sure." With that Maria immediately swung the car around and headed toward her own home.

"There is one more problem," Flora stammered, "about attending church with you."

"What is it?" Noemi asked.

"I-I-I don't own any dresses. I will have to come in slacks."

"Hey," Maria waved aside Flora's obstruction. "That's no problem. We'll just be glad to have you there."

Within minutes the car stopped in front of a modest stucco home. "Wait right here," Maria instructed as she bounded from the car. Within seconds she returned, waving the promised gift in the air.

Maria opened the car door and handed the book to Flora.

Flora trembled as she took it. "Thank you," she whispered as she ran her fingers over the textured surface.

Later, in the privacy of her room, Flora traced the gold letters on the leather binding—*SANTA BIBLIA*, Holy Bible. Reverently, she caressed the onionskin pages. Then she read snatches here and there and at last stumbled onto Revelation 19:8. There she read about the white linen robes which are called the righteousness of the saints.

Exhaustion and the realization that Hillary would soon be waking up, finally drove Flora to her bed. Still clutching her treasure close to her heart, she turned off her lamp next to her bed. As her eyes adjusted to the darkness, she waited for the nightly visit from "Grandma Marta." But the being in the pink, floor-length nightgown did not appear. Too sleepy to wonder why, she drifted off into a peaceful sleep, the first she'd had since she was a young child.

The girl started awake as the early morning sun filtered in through her window. A glance at her alarm clock told her that she'd not only slept peacefully, but she'd overslept too. She sensed an unaccustomed weight on her chest—the Bible! A smile wreathed Flora's face. Carlotta's curse—had the Bible broken Carlotta's curse? Did it have power stronger than that of the witch? Flora slipped into her robe and hurried to the nursery to answer Hillary's cries.

Chapter 13
A Taste of Heaven

Flora paced back and forth in front of the Foss estate, the Bible tucked under her right arm. Her navy-blue polyester pants sported a fresh crease. With her free hand, she picked at an invisible spot on the sleeve of her red and white checkered top. Between Wednesday night and Saturday morning, she had spent every spare moment reading her new Bible. She had even read Hillary to sleep each afternoon instead of singing. Even though she found reading hard to master, she persisted.

Impatient, Flora ran to the edge of the circle drive and looked up the street then down. "What if I misunderstood the time and get there too late?" She frowned as a new, more disturbing thought surfaced. "What if Maria forgot me?" She sighed with relief when Maria's green Mustang appeared in view.

"Hola." Flora hopped into the car beside Maria. "Where's Noemi?"

"She'll be at church." Maria shifted the car into gear. "Sorry I was late. My car has been giving me trouble. My Dad thinks it's the timing."

Maria glanced over at Flora. "I'm glad to see you have your Bible with you. Have you had time to look it over since Wednesday?"

"Oh yes. The only time I don't read it is when Grandma Foss is around. I don't think she would approve, since she doesn't believe in Jesus."

"They do believe in the Old Testament, you know," affirmed Maria.

"Yes, but it is the New Testament I like best—especially the stories about Jesus," Flora told her friend.

"Yes, the gospels are easier to understand," concluded Maria.

"Gospels?" Flora asked.

"The stories about Jesus," Maria explained.

"You know," said Flora, "since you gave me the Bible, I have slept the entire night, every night, undisturbed. That's the first time that has happened since I was a child."

"I don't understand," said Maria, as she zigzagged through the morning traffic.

"Oh, it's the greatest thing that's ever happened. The spirit of my Grandmother used to appear to me every night, but this hasn't happened a single time since you gave me the Bible." Flora explained, then told her friend about Carlotta's curse and the nightly visitations of Grandma Marta's ghost.

Thirty minutes later, Flora completed her story. "So you see, the power of the Bible is greater than Carlotta's curse."

As the car pulled into the church parking lot, Maria explained, "Flora, the power is in God, the Author of the Book, not in the onionskin paper and leather of the book."

Sabbath School was in session by the time the girls entered the vestibule where Noemi stood waiting. An older woman greeted Flora and Maria and invited Flora to sign the guestbook.

Suddenly Flora paled. A hauntingly familiar melody came from beyond the swinging doors:

> Shall we gather at the river
> Where bright angel feet have trod
> With its crystal tide forever
> Flowing by the throne of God?

Then the chorus:

> Yes, we'll gather at the river,
> The beautiful, the beautiful river;
> Gather with the saints at the river
> That flows from the throne of God.

Flora recalled Señor Ortega's words, "You become a saint when you join the family of God." A wisp of a smile traced across Flora's face as a sense of peace flooded through her. Tears slid unbidden down her face, and she heard Maria and Noemi asking her why she was crying.

"Are you in pain?" Noemi whispered.

"No," Flora said, pointed toward the sanctuary, "I want to go inside."

The girls slipped quietly into a pew as the song ended. After opening exercises ended, the Sabbath School superintendent dismissed those present for lesson study.

The three girls entered a small room behind the main sanctuary filled with other youth. Flora listened to the Sabbath School teacher tell of the beauties of heaven. Excited over what she heard, she glanced about, expecting the same thrill on the faces of the other young people. Instead, two girls on one side of her sat looking at pictures in each other's wallets. Behind her, a number of boys slouched in their chairs, obviously bored. Another was sleeping. Even Marie and Noemi were whispering to one another.

"How can these kids hear such exciting news and not respond?" she wondered.

A bell rang and the teacher ended the class with prayer. Flora followed Noemi and Marie back into the auditorium. This time when she entered, Flora inspected the room critically. There were no candles, no crucifix above the pulpit, no vacant-eyed idols sentineling the walls. "Such a strange church," she thought.

The announcement period and opening exercises floated past Flora as she studied the church and the other worshipers. She noted their happy, smiling faces and their expensive clothing. "I am too ugly, too dirty to be with these people. They are the saints Señor Ortega told about—not me. I don't belong!"

A short, balding man stepped up to the podium. "That's Elder Torrez. He's neat," Maria whispered.

Flora liked the man's rich, resonant voice. "All children may come forward for the children's story," he announced.

Tears welled up in Flora's eyes as the younger boys and girls made their way to the front of the church. "They're so beautiful," she thought, "so innocent." As she watched, she remembered her own childhood. She felt empty, somehow robbed. She glanced around at the proud smiles on the parents' faces. She'd never seen such pride and love on her own mother's face.

After the children returned to their seats, the minister began his sermon. He told the story of Jesus and the woman at the well. "A daughter of Abraham became, that day, a daughter of the heavenly King," he explained. "She became as pure and clean as an innocent babe." Then he continued with the story of the woman taken in adultery.

As his theme unfolded, Flora knew he was speaking directly to her. "The Master didn't condemn the woman. He didn't broadcast her many sins. He said, 'Go and sin no more.'" The man's gaze swept across the congregation. "So simple, so direct, so compassionate. Today, the Master says to you, to me, 'Go and sin no more.'"

Flora wiped her cheek in an effort to stop the tears slipping down her cheek. She sensed that her friends were frowning at her, but she couldn't help herself. Her thoughts wandered on.

The minister continued speaking, ". . . clean, totally clean. And, like the woman at the well, the former prostitute became as innocent and clean as she was the day she was born, for, after all, she'd been reborn."

Flora ached to understand the preacher's words. "How can someone be born again?" She'd felt dirty and unworthy for so many years.

"You can experience this cleansing today, brothers and sisters. Jesus longs to wash away your sins," Pastor Torrez continued. "He yearns to give you a glistening white robe of righteousness. He is eager to take you home with Him to heaven. Through His power you, too, can become a son or a daughter of God. In John 1:12, we read . . ."

Suddenly Flora saw visions of the coveted bride doll flashed into her consciousness; she heard the nun's white robes swishing along the cluttered halls of her mind. A moment of pain and anger stabbed at her heart, then Señor Ortega's voice replaced the pastor's. "As many as believe on His name—to them gave He power to become a son—or daughter—of God."

One by one, the pieces of her past began to fall into place. A new thought surfaced. "Could this Jesus have been leading me all along? Could this be the power Grandma Marta said I possess?" All of a sudden such a possibility disturbed Flora. She reacted to it and vowed to sever all ties with God. After all, wasn't He the source of her disappointment?

A battle raged within her as the congregation stood for closing prayer. "I don't understand. A saint . . . can I really ever become a real live saint?"

Maria nudged Flora's arm. "It's time to go," the girl whispered, directing Flora's attention to the deacon standing patiently at the end of their row. When a number of people shook Flora's hand and invited her back again, there was no doubt in her mind she'd be back every chance she got.

Maria's mother, Señora Leon, invited Flora to Sabbath dinner.

"Sabbath dinner?" Flora thought of the times she'd wished she could join the Foss's Sabbath meal. "Me? I'd love to," she answered, her eyes alive with anticipation. The girl smiled to herself. At least, thanks to Grandma Foss, she knew the traditions for Sabbath etiquette and wouldn't make any stupid mistakes.

Maria and Flora followed the Leon family car home in the Mustang. "How does your mother shape the challah?" Flora asked.

"What?" Maria gave her new friend a strange look.

"The challah, you know, the Sabbath bread?"

Maria stopped the car in front of her home. "I have no idea what you're talking about. My mom makes her own wheat bread, but I never heard it called . . . What did you call it?"

"Challah—the Shabbat bread."

"Oh no. That must be a Jewish custom, not a Christian one," Maria explained.

"Oh!" Flora followed Maria inside. "Perhaps I won't know the customs after all," she mumbled to herself.

Señora Leon heated dinner in the oven, while Flora helped Maria and her younger sister Liza, set the table. She knew Grandma Foss would disapprove of keeping the Sabbath in this manner.

When Señora Leon announced it was time to eat, the family gathered about the table. They bowed their heads as Señor Leon blessed the food. At first, the family were curious about their guest. Flora politely answered their barrage of questions. As the attention on her lessened, Flora was surprised by the change in topic.

"I wish Pastor Torrez would try a new theme in his sermons once in a while," Señor Leon commented. "Every week he preaches about the forgiveness of sin."

"Well, a lot of people in that church need just such a sermon," Señora Leon commented, then seemed to change the subject. "Did you notice Patricia Saen's wedding ring?"

"No big deal," Maria interrupted. "She's wears gobs of jewelry at work. But I was surprised at Antonia's dress. The neckline would make the imps blush."

"Well, dear," Señora Leon added knowingly, "she's always been a little loose, you know."

"By the way, have Noemi's parents settled their differences yet?" Marie's father asked. "Imagine, arguing at the church picnic—how tasteless!"

Flora listened, unable to believe what she was hearing. A heavy sadness settled over her. She'd been so blessed by the minister's words. And the people all seemed so pure and holy. Had she been deceived?

Later that afternoon, Maria offered to drive Flora home. On the way, Maria asked, "I've been dying to know. Why did you cry, in church, I mean? Were you unhappy?"

"Oh no," Flora replied. "One does not need to feel pain to cry."

"I suppose . . ." Maria mumbled, accelerating into the traffic. The girls didn't talk during the ride home. Each seemed lost in her own thoughts.

Before Flora climbed out at the Foss's house, Maria offered to take her to church each Sabbath. "I-I-I think I'd like that," Flora replied.

When she reached the confines of her room, Flora sank into the easy chair and kicked off her shoes. Her head ached from all she'd seen and heard. She'd been so thrilled with the promise of forgiveness and of becoming a full-fledged saint. At the same time she felt disappointment. How did it all fit together? It was confusing. "Am I being deceived—just like Mama is with Carlotta?" Doubts wrestled to oust the beautiful message she'd heard.

Chapter 14
Friends From Home

Flora read aloud from Ecclesiastes 9:5. "The living know that they shall die: but the dead know not any thing."

"You see, Flora, the Bible teaches just as you suspected," Pastor Torrez explained. "Your Grandma Marta couldn't have come back to visit you after she died."

"But she was real," Flora argued. "I felt her touch my arm."

Pastor Torrez smiled and nodded. "Oh, the being you saw was definitely real, but that doesn't mean it was your grandmother. I think you'll find the answer to all your questions in this book."

Flora took the book, *The Great Controversy*, and read the Spanish title, *El Conflicto de los Siglos*.

The minister tapped the cover of the burgundy-covered book. "If you read what this author has to say, reading the Bible texts as you go, you will discover the source of Carlotta's power and her curse."

Flora glided out of the pastor's study, relieved to know he hadn't been rejecting Grandma Marta as she had sometimes feared.

Within two days, Flora had read the entire volume and yearned to read more. Each Sabbath, the Leons and Pastor Torrez gave her books to read. At home, Grandma Foss continued delivering her "sermons" in Yiddish. Once, Flora showed Grandma Foss a small picture of Jesus Señora Leon had given her.

"Jesus," Flora said, "He is God."

Grandma shook her finger in Flora's face and scolded. "No! Jesus a man—not Jehovah—just a man!" After that Flora treasured her discoveries in her heart.

Flora was delighted when her classmate and friend Alejandra accepted her invitation to attend church. From the first week,

Alejandra eagerly accepted everything she learned. Now Flora had someone with whom she could share her excitement over each new discovery. Alejandra gave Flora an escape from spending every Sabbath at either Maria's home or Noemi's. The two families had established a routine of alternately inviting her home for dinner each Sabbath. Flora would have enjoyed these visits if the families hadn't indulged in cannibalizing each other over the dinner table. This troubled her. The actions of these people didn't square with all the wonderful things she was learning.

Much to Flora's dismay, Alejandra learned and accepted the truths much faster than she did. Some of Flora's studies continued to be difficult for her. It was as if, somewhere along the way, the switch to learning inside her brain had been turned off. The scars resulting from years of physical and sexual abuse had stunted her reasoning power. She couldn't seem to retain what she heard or read. At times, she wondered if she'd ever be able to learn and understand the beautiful things she was reading.

Slowly, imperceptibly, her mind cleared. Señor Ortega's teachings also began to make sense. And the clearer her mind became, the more excited Flora grew over her new-found faith. She couldn't keep it to herself. She wanted to tell everyone.

After learning about baptism, Flora decided to be baptized. She compared this rite to marrying Jesus—just like the nuns did when they took the veil. In her letter home that week, Flora described her happiness at finding Jesus, and asked Mama's permission to be baptized. Her answer came by return mail.

"If you go through with this blasphemous scheme," her mother wrote, "you will no longer be my daughter. You are working with the devil!"

The scar tissue built up from her abused childhood left her fearful of making any decision that might displease others, especially her mother. Flora was afraid to continue with her plans.

The inconsistency and backbiting she witnessed on Sabbath afternoons at Maria's and Noemi's homes began to fill her mind. Flora began to notice cliques in the church that regularly picked each other apart. She compared the simple navy-blue shirtwaist dress she'd purchased especially for church with the fancy clothes her church friends wore and wondered, "Maybe I really don't belong there. Maybe Mama is right. Maybe I haven't found the true church after all."

Flora stopped attending church. A nagging restlessness replaced the peace she'd experienced. With her mother so vehemently opposed, Flora began to distrust her earlier decision, yet enviously watched Alejandra grow in the faith. She longed to do the same, yet seemed to hold back, so that whenever Alejandra tried to share her happiness, Flora shrank away. The church became a barrier between them.

So, when Paulina Lucero, a native of El Salvador, joined the night class Flora was attending and took an interest in her, the homesick girl responded enthusiastically. To be with someone from home—could anything be better?

The thirty-five-year-old woman showed a motherly interest in the girl. "Your story is similar to mine," Paulina confided. "My stepfather beat me too. He said I didn't earn my keep. That's why I am here in Los Angeles instead of El Salvador."

Flora listened as Paulina told of the brawls in her stepfather's bar and the beatings she'd received in her mother's sleazy brothel attached to the bar. "No matter how many johns I fleeced in a night, it wasn't enough for Luis," Paulina explained.

Johns? Fleeced? Flora didn't understand such expressions, but she felt Paulina's humiliation and pain. Flora reached out to comfort her new friend. Paulina accepted Flora's compassion avidly. Their friendship deepened.

Flora spent more and more of her free time with Paulina. When Alejandra met Paulina, she took an instant dislike to the older woman. "She dresses and acts like a, a . . ." The girl searched for the right English term, "A hooker."

"A hooker? What is a hooker?"

"You know—a prostitute—a woman who sells herself to men."

"No way!" Flora bristled with anger. "She is my friend. You are jealous because I am spending time with her instead of you. Or maybe that church of yours is turning you into a snob."

"Church of mine?" Alejandra responded. "It was your church before it became mine."

"Maybe, but I'm not so sure that it is my church anymore," Flora muttered, turning away from her friend. "I'm not sure of anything anymore."

A few weeks into their friendship, Paulina suggested that Flora quit work at the Foss's and find a better-paying job, and that the two of them find an apartment to share. Flora was thrilled with the idea. Their search didn't last long, and soon they outfitted a small, two bedroom apartment with Flora's modest savings.

Flora missed the Fosses, especially Hillary. But she realized that the larger paycheck she received from the laundry would supply her with a place of her own, or at least one she could share with Paulina.

Flora thought of Paulina—so tender and caring, so willing to listen as Flora relived the horrors of her childhood. It was reasonable for her to turn over her paycheck to her friend each week instead of sending it to her mother in El Salvador.

When Alejandra learned Flora gave Paulina her entire paycheck each week, she bristled. "You're giving all your money to that woman? How can you be so stupid? She's using you One of these days you will learn not to trust everyone that comes along. You will learn to say No. You will learn to defend your rights—if you survive long enough!"

"Oh, Alejandra," Flora shook her head sadly, "you don't understand."

"I'm afraid I *do* understand," retorted Alejandra.

"No, she is my friend. She is from home."

"She is deceiving you, and you are letting her do it!"

Flora stared at the floor tiles, then lifted her head to meet Alejandra's concerned gaze. "Please try to understand. You have a family; I don't. Paulina is like a mother to me. I need her."

Alejandra ran exasperated fingers through her bangs. "And at what expense, Flora?"

"What do you mean?" Flora recountered.

Alejandra paused. "Oh, I don't know. Do me one favor, will you?"

Confused by the sudden tears that sprang into Alejandra's brown eyes, Flora nodded. "If anything goes wrong," said Alejandra, "I'll be here to help."

From the moment Flora met Lila and Gustavo, two of Paulina's friends from El Salvador, she didn't like them, especially the lean, sinewy Gustavo. Every time he glanced her way, icy shivers traveled up and down her spine. His cold penetrating gaze seemed to strip her bare. His sneering laugh brought unwelcome visions of Arturo. She determined never to be alone with him.

One evening, Flora stood watching as Paulina drew a thin blue line across her eyelid. "How about going bar-hopping with us tonight?"

"You know I don't drink or dance," Flora answered.

"That's good. It would really help if you learned to drive, so you could drive us from club to club," Paulina suggested. "Having you drive would be safer than having Gustavo drive after he's had too many drinks."

"I don't know." Flora demurred, hating to disappoint her friend.

Paulina puckered her lips and applied a coat of hot-pink lipstick. "Aw, come on," she teased, "loosen up! You're not in the old country now. And I'd really appreciate it if you'd go along."

Flora relented. "OK, I'll go—but just to ride along."

"Great!" exclaimed Paulina. "Here, let me do something with your hair. And your face. I'll just add a little blush here and midnight blue on your eyelids . . ."

"Hey, I just agreed to ride along!" Flora protested weakly. By the time Paulina finished, Flora hardly recognized her neon image reflected in the mirror.

Flora allowed herself to be squeezed into a skimpy little dress of vibrant blue satin and matching pumps. Lila and Gustavo arrived before Flora could do anything about the changes. The two women fluttered about the stunned girl, cooing at the transformations Paulina had wrought. Meanwhile Gustavo stood off to one side, admiring the scenery, his greedy eyes following Flora as she practice walking in spiked heels.

"Paulina, I feel stupid dressed like this."

"Nonsense!" The woman waved away Flora's protests. "You were an ugly duckling just waiting for someone to turn you into a beautiful swan."

Flora lifted her hand to object, but was quickly swept from the apartment and into the waiting automobile.

Chapter 15
Evening Intruder

Alejandra slipped a second quarter into the pop machine and tapped the button. An ice-cold can of ginger ale dropped onto the tray. "So where's Paulina tonight?" she inquired.

"She's partying with Lila and Gustavo," Flora replied.

"And you didn't go along?" Alejandra's eyes widened in mock surprise.

"I can't afford to miss class."

"I'm worried about you, Flora."

"Look," Flora defended, "when I go out with them, it's to drive them home safely, that's all. I don't drink, smoke, or dance."

"I'm sorry," sighed Alejandra, "but I just can't help worrying."

"I'm sorry too." Flora placed her hand on her friend's shoulder. "And I'll have to admit, sometimes the pressure gets pretty bad—especially when it comes to dancing.

"Oh?"

Flora shrugged her shoulders. "They say I could become rich dancing in Paulina's stepfather's bar back home. The three of them are planning to return to San Salvador to work in his bar. She says El Salvadoran men pay big money for a woman who has lived in the United States. They want me to go with them. I won't though."

Alejandra suddenly changed the subject. "Did I tell you that my entire family is attending church—thanks to you? If you hadn't invited me that first week . . ."

Flora scooped her books off the desktop. "I think I'm going to leave a little early tonight."

"Wait," Alejandra called. "You seem to be running from me—and from God. I'm here to help you. I care about you."

"I-I-I can't," stammered Flora. "I'd like to start going back to church; I'm not good enough to go to church. I'm only the same filthy little girl I've always been."

"That's nonsense!" Alejandra countered. "You need to talk with Pastor Torrez."

"No!" Flora whirled away from her friend. "Church doesn't work for me, OK?" Tears blinded her as she hurried from the building.

When she reached her apartment, Flora found Paulina and Lila sitting in the kitchen, discussing their trip to El Salvador.

Paulina glanced at Flora and shook her head. "I feel like I'm cutting off my right arm leaving you here all alone. Why don't you come with us?"

"Yeah," Lila agreed, eyeing Flora critically, "with your neat little body, you could really rake in the dough."

Perspiration broke out of Flora's forehead as Lila's words sank in. *"NO!"* she responded firmly. "NO I-I-I could never . . ."

"Why don't you just give yourself a chance?" Lila suggested.

Repelled by Lila's suggestion, Flora blurted, "NO! Never! I do not want any man."

Paulina placed her hand on Flora's shoulder in a friendly manner. "Now, Lila, stop teasing Flora." Then turning to Flora, "of course, you could never do what Lila suggests. Now dancing, you could do that, couldn't you?"

"Please, Paulina," pleaded Flora, "must you really go back? What is there in El Salvador for you?"

Paulina threw her head back and laughed. "Money, my dear—filthy, dirty money."

"But you have my money, all that I earn," Flora pointed out. "And you have your money. Isn't that enough?"

"Sweetheart," Paulina began, "what we make here is chicken feed compared to what we can earn in San Salvador."

Flora glanced from Paulina to Lila and shook her head. With a sigh, she went to her room, took her Bible off the night stand, and opened it. She leafed through the Gospel of John, her favorite book. Had it really been so long since she'd eagerly eaten every word in this book? It still kept Carlotta's demons away at night. An unexplained chill grasped Flora's heart. She gazed about the room. Everything was as she'd left it that morning. Yet, she seemed to sense evil lurking in the shadows.

Throughout the next day, her mind flitted between her conversation with Paulina and her talk with Alejandra. At the end of Flora's shift, Paulina called.

"Flora honey," the woman purred, "I'd appreciate it if you would tidy up the apartment this evening. I won't be home tonight. I'll see you after work on Friday, OK?"

Later, when Flora returned to the apartment, her feet ached. "I'll take a short nap first," she thought as she surveyed the living room—last night's newspaper lay strewn across the couch along with empty beer cans. The breakfast dishes still littered the kitchen table.

Flora tossed her navy jacket, and beige shoulder-strap purse on a chair and walked into her darkened bedroom. Too tired to turn on the light, she shed her jeans and blouse and slipped into a cotton robe she'd left at the foot of her bed. With a toss of her head, Flora swung her long braid over her shoulder, undid the tie at the end, and shook her hair free, then slid beneath the bed covers.

Flora drifted off to sleep. Restless, she flung her left arm across the far side of the bed. It thudded against something solid—a body! Someone had sneaked into her bed! Before she could react, a rough, calloused hand forced her head back against the pillow while the other hand grabbed a fistful of her hair. The odor of stale alcohol filled her nostrils as her assailant uttered a low, guttural laugh and tried to open her robe's closure.

Flora screamed. Suddenly she was a young child again, fighting against the repulsive Arturo. "No, no, not again," she wailed, turning her face from side to side in an effort to escape the intruder's noxious breath.

"Oh, playing hard to get, are you," the man growled. "It's OK; I like 'em that way."

"No, I can't live through this again, Lord," she cried out. "Please give me strength. Please, Father, help me."

Suddenly one of her hands broke free. Viciously she raked her nails the length of her attacker's face. Bellowing in pain, the man released his grip on her hair. In that instant, Flora bounded from the bed.

She had reached the bedroom door when the man wrestled her to the floor from behind. Her face slammed against the cold tile. She kicked and screamed as he struggled to restrain her. Almost instinctively, she reached over her shoulder and gouged his left eyeball. With another yelp of pain the man released the frightened girl and cursed his would-be victim.

Free from his clutches, Flora bolted from the apartment screaming and ran across the hall to the landlord's quarters. It wasn't until the startled landlord's face registered shock that Flora became aware of her state of undress.

"Please, Señor Harris," the hysterical girl sobbed, "there is a man—in my apartment!"

The landlord rushed across the hall to investigate, while his wife gathered the sobbing girl into her arms. Minutes later, Mr. Harris returned. "Whoever it was has gone."

"Are you sure?" Flora asked tearfully.

"You and Nora come with me, and we'll check together," the landlord suggested," motioning Flora and his wife to follow. Then he asked, "Did you recognize the man? Were your doors locked?"

"I-I-I'm not sure," Flora stammered, "I mean, I didn't recognize the man, but I think there was something familiar about him. And yes, I locked the door when I left for work, it was locked when I returned home, and I locked it behind me when I went in. Why?"

"Well, I found no evidence of a forced entry."

"How could that be possible!" exclaimed Flora. "Only Paulina and I have keys." Now a new anxiety began to nibble at Flora's mind. "If he has a key, he could come back."

Afraid to be alone, she telephoned Alejandra.

"Alejandra? Can you come over to my apartment right away? I need you. Something—something terrible has happened."

Within minutes Alejandra arrived and Flora relived the nightmare struggle with the intruder. When she finished, Alejandra asked, "Did you recognize the man?"

"No," said Flora, "but there was something about him that seemed familiar."

"Alejandra," Flora asked, "why do these things have to happen to me? Am I to blame because of something I've done wrong?"

"Flora, it's not your fault."

"But I feel it is. I feel filthy, dirty. I *must* have done something wrong, or these things wouldn't happen to me. I must be to blame."

"Flora, don't think that. Remember, God answered your prayer. He helped you escape from your assailant."

"God didn't help me," Flora argued. "My nails helped me escape. God has abandoned me."

Hours later, an exhausted Flora stretched out on the sofa.

Alejandra settled herself in the large overstuffed chair and began reading aloud to Flora from the Psalms: "The Lord is my shepherd, I shall not want. . . ."

The sound of Alejandra's reassuring voice calmed Flora. As she drifted in and out of sleep, she could hear her friend reading: "wash me and I shall be whiter than snow. . . ."

After a while Flora roused enough to hear and remember the words from Proverbs: "Trust in the Lord with all thine heart; and lean not unto thine own understanding. In all thy ways acknowledge Him, and He shall direct thy paths."

"Maybe that's my mistake," she thought. "Maybe I've been trusting the wrong people."

The sun had barely reached the valley floor when the telephone jangled the two girls awake. Flora reached over to answer it.

"Flora?" Lila's sugary voice came over the line. "Did you have a nice time last night?"

Flora ran her fingers through her tangled hair. "Why?" she asked.

"Did you stay at the apartment?"

"Y-e-s," Flora replied slowly. "Why do you ask?" She could hear muffled snickers in the background. She heard the phone click, then a dial tone.

"That's strange."

Turning to Alejandra, Flora repeated the conversation.

Alejandra's dark eyes flashed in anger. "I don't like what she said. Something's fishy. I don't know what it is yet, but something definitely stinks. You mustn't stay here anymore. Why don't you come home with me?" she invited. "What if that creep comes back?"

"I have to work all day. Paulina will be here when I get home tonight, and then I'll be all right," Flora explained. "You're a true friend, Alejandra, and I want you to know I appreciate you."

Alejandra heaved a sigh of resignation. "As you like, but just remember, I am only a phone call away."

Chapter 16
Escape by Fire

Flora stepped out into the noonday sun and stretched her aching muscles. "Maybe Paulina has returned to the apartment," she thought as she crossed the street to the pay phone. "I'll give her a call and find out."

The phone rang several times before Paulina answered.

"Well, Flora darling," the woman soothed, "did you have a nice time last night?"

"What are you talking about?" Flora snapped.

"I-I just wondered," Paulina stammered in feigned surprise. "You were at the apartment all evening, weren't you?"

"Yes, I was there," Flora admitted with a touch of bitterness. "I need to talk with you. Will you be home when I get there?"

"W-e-l-l-l, what about?" the woman drawled suspiciously, then, "Yes, I'll be here."

"Good," Flora responded, "because we really need to talk."

As the afternoon sped by, Flora thought of Alejandra's warnings, but finally decided, "I can handle this myself."

After work, Flora took a crowded bus for home. When she got off, she walked up the street curb reluctantly, climbed the front stairs and entered the hallway to her apartment.

The familiar sounds in the tenement building soothed her edgy nerves. Flora inserted the key into the lock and opened the door. "Hola," she called, "I'm home."

The living room was bathed in candlelight. Candles of varying sizes and colors decorated every flat surface. The warm, seductive tones of Paulina's favorite singer crooned from the stereo.

"Hi, honey." Paulina sat lotus style on the sofa, a lighted cigarette in one hand and a half-empty wine glass in the other. "Come on in; we're having a party."

"A-a party?" Flora gulped. Her heart sank at the sight of Lila draped across the arm and seat of an armchair—her face flushed from alcohol.

"Hey, Lila," slurred Paulina, "go get Flora a drink."

"No," Flora interrupted, "nothing for me."

"Nonsense." Lila unwound her legs and sauntered toward the kitchen. "Want a Coke or a root beer?"

"A root beer will be fine," Flora answered, turning to hang her jacket in the front closet.

"S-o-o-o, you had a quiet evening at home last night, eh?" Paulina giggled.

"No, not exactly," Flora answered.

"Poor baby," Paulina sneered condescendingly. "Isn't it about time the baby becomes a big girl?"

Flora stared at the stranger she'd considered almost to be her second mother. Nausea swept through her.

"Quit staring and sit down," Paulina growled, "You make me nervous." Flora obeyed.

Lila returned with a tumbler of root beer. "Here ya' go, sugar," she said, giving the tumbler to Flora.

Flora thanked her and took a sip of the dark brown liquid.

Paulina leaned forward and tapped the ashes from her cigarette on the edge of an ashtray. "Lila and I are leaving for San Salvador next week. A friend of Gustavo's has a six-passenger plane. We reserved a seat for you too."

"No," Flora replied firmly, her voice rising in intensity at the mention of Gustavo, "I won't be going with you."

Paulina tipped her head to one side. A quizzical smile played at the corners of her lips. "Perhaps . . . perhaps," she said mysteriously. "But for now, just drink your soda."

Suddenly a wave of nausea swept over Flora. She felt overheated, her breath came in short gasps. She looked toward Paulina but couldn't bring her face into focus. A silly grin spread across Paulina's face and seemed to disappear into her hairline.

"I-I-I, don't feel so good," Flora complained.

"You're just upset about being left behind," Paulina suggested.

Flora glanced across the room. Instead of one Lila she saw two, holding matching wine glasses in a salute to her. The voices of more than a dozen Paulinas and Lilas echoed throughout the room. Their words didn't make sense.

"Let her drink a little more; then we'll turn her over to Gustavo," Paulina announced matter-of-factly. "Then let's get her on that plane before the drug wears off."

The glass tumbler slid to the floor as Flora fought to lift her head. She could hear Paulina calling her name. Her voice seemed to echo down a long tunnel. Flora felt someone guide her to her feet. "Time for beddy-bye, little one," the voice purred.

"I need to sleep," Flora admitted.

"Come on," Paulina coaxed, "one foot in front of the other."

The inside of Flora's mouth felt swollen and dry. She fought to open her eyes. She succeeded just enough to see Gustavo leaning insolently against the bedroom doorjamb. One eye was swollen and partially shut. Long red scratches ran the length of his craggy face.

Suddenly the pieces of the puzzle fell into place. Gustavo was her mysterious attacker, and Paulina's wicked scheme to kidnap her for purposes of prostitution became clear.

"Oh heavenly Father, please, please help me," Flora mumbled, her words slurring over one another. Fighting the fog that seemed determined to engulf her, Flora snapped her head back. Her mind partially cleared.

Suddenly, a new terror replaced the old. She saw angry flames leaping through the kitchen doorway into the living room. The entire kitchen was a blazing inferno.

"Fire!" screamed Flora. "Fire!"

Paulina and Lila gasped as Gustavo shouted, "Go call the fire department." Grabbing a blanket from the bedroom, he began beating the flames.

The women released Flora's arms and ran to help extinguish the blaze. Mustering her last shreds of consciousness, Flora stumbled out of the building onto the street. The fresh night air revived her. Suddenly she sensed her need to put as much distance between herself and the apartment as possible, and stumbled on.

"One foot then the other," she repeated.

Eventually she found herself at Alejandra's home.

Even though it was past bedtime, Flora knocked. When Alejandra opened it, tears of gratitude streamed down the girl's face as she burst into the Martinez home. "Help me!" she cried, throwing herself in her startled friend's arms, "Help me."

Señor Martinez helped Flora to the sofa, while his wife rushed to get the girl a glass of cold water.

"Have you eaten?" asked Señora Martinez as she handed the young woman the tumbler of water.

"No, I-I-I can't eat right now," answered Flora, her hands shaking uncontrollably. "I am too nauseated and sleepy."

"What happened?" Señor Martinez's asked

"I-I-I'm too sleepy. I can't . . ." Flora's voice thickened to a stop.

"You mustn't fall asleep, Flora," Señor Martinez insisted. "You might never wake up. What did you take?"

"I don't know," she slurred.

"Talk, Flora," Alejandra insisted, slapping her friend's face.

"I can't."

"You must!" Señor Martinez shook Flora's shoulders.

Later, when Señor Martinez returned to the parlor, he insisted on taking Flora to the hospital. But by the time they arrived there, the drugs had been sufficiently eliminated from her system, and the doctor couldn't tell what drug she'd ingested, so he sent her home with Señor Martinez.

Back at Alejandra's house Señora Martinez greeted them with some good news. "Flora, I talked with Molly (Alejandra's older sister), and she has invited you to stay with her until you can find another place of your own. Stay with us tonight and tomorrow night, we'll pick up your things at your apartment."

As Flora pondered Paulina's wicked scheme, she felt betrayed. "She was my friend; I loved her," the girl wept quietly into her pillow. "I'm dirty, filthy dirty," she sobbed. "I am worth nothing, less than nothing. O God, how can You say You love me? There is no one in this world who loves me, no one."

Hours later Flora awoke with a throbbing headache. It was Sabbath morning. Alejandra urged Flora to get up and accompany her to church, but Flora demurred. She said she wasn't feeling well. But Alejandra wouldn't take No for an answer. "Come on. Either you're going to church with me, or I'm staying here with you. I'm not going to leave you here alone."

Flora agreed to go to church with Alejandra. While she showered, Alejandra laid out some clothes for her to wear.

Flora was overwhelmed by the warm greeting she received as she entered the church. When Pastor Torrez began speaking, her heart began to beat faster as old familiar feelings began to return. In the same tender tones she remembered so well, the minister retold the story of the woman at the well and the prostitute dragged in and thrown at Jesus' feet. The sermon stirred her heart even more than it had the first time. When Pastor Torrez made an altar call, Flora knew it was meant for her. Without hesitation, she stood to her feet.

"I know I don't deserve Your love and forgiveness, Father, but I'm accepting it anyway," she prayed silently.

Flora spent Sabbath afternoon with the Martinez's. At sundown, the family gathered again for worship. Flora couldn't believe the changes that had taken place in the Martinez home since the family had begun attending church.

Night had fallen by the time Flora, Alejandra, and Señor Martinez climbed into the family station wagon and drove to the apartment to pick up Flora's things. When they got there, Flora was surprised. The apartment building was still standing!

"I don't know what condition things will be in," she warned as she walked up the front steps with her friends.

"Hola?" she called after she unlocked and opened the door. Her voice echoed off the high-ceilinged walls. "I guess no one's home," she said, reaching inside and flipping the wall switch.

Flora's breath caught in her throat as the room flooded with light. She rushed from one room to the next. To her amazement there was not the least evidence of a fire. She couldn't believe her eyes. The kitchen was in perfect condition—not a burn, not a water spot, not a whiff of smoke!

Footsteps in the living room caused Flora, Alejandra, and her father to turn in surprise. It was Mr. Harris, the landlord.

"Where did they go?" Flora asked.

"They cleared out of here Friday evening," the landlord explained. "They claimed there was a fire, but it was all in their minds. Those people were stoned when they left."

Although she'd miss her precious Bible and her treasure box, Flora felt relieved to know that Paulina and her two friends were out of her life forever. Without a single possession, Flora suddenly felt wealthy. She had her life and her freedom.

"Señor Martinez," said Flora, "could you arrange for me to speak with Pastor Torrez soon?"

"I'll call him when we get back to the house," he assured her.

Chapter 17
Victory Over Defeat

Flora studied the Bible with Pastor Torrez and readily accepted the Bible teachings he presented. But trust in God's love and His forgiveness came hard.

"I hear what you say about forgiveness, Pastor, but I still don't feel clean. I don't feel I can ever be a saint."

"Flora," the pastor began, "you do not need to feel forgiven to be forgiven. You do not need to feel like a saint to be one. It is your faith in God's promises and power, not your feelings, that guarantee your place in God's family."

Flora shook her head. "I don't know."

"You must step out in faith, Flora," he urged. "Believe God's promises, even though you cannot see or feel the difference."

Flora thought about the minister's words and made her decision to be baptized. During the last of her baptismal classes, she asked a question that had plagued her for a very long time.

"Pastor, all those years—what was the power I possessed? I know it was real," she said. "Grandma Marta warned me to guard it. Carlotta tried to control it. And Mama was determined to exploit it."

Pastor Torrez looked at Flora intently. "Do you really want my opinion?" he asked.

Flora nodded.

"Since God knows the end from the beginning, He knew you would one day choose to join His family—to become His daughter. So, in order to protect you from the powers of evil bent on your destruction," Pastor Torrez paused, then continued, "I believe He sent His Holy Spirit with an extra measure of protection until you could make that choice."

A smile formed about the edges of Flora's lips as she accepted the pastor's answer to her question. "You mean, when I became God's daughter, He became my Father?" she said. "I never really had a father, you know."

"Here's a text that might bring you encouragement, Flora," Pastor Torrez replied, turning to Galatians 4:6, NIV, giving it a personal application. "Because you are [a daughter], God sent the Spirit of His son into [your] heart, the Spirit who calls out, 'Abba, Father.' So you are no longer a slave, but a [daughter], ... God has made you also an heir." The minister handed the Bible to Flora, giving her time to read the words for herself. "Do you know what 'Abba' means, Flora? It means Father, Daddy."

"Daddy?" Flora repeated breathlessly. Tears came unbidden to her eyes. "Daddy? Alejandra calls her father, 'Daddy.' "

Flora considered this new concept. The term *father* evoked images of harshness, unyielding cruelty, abandonment. But *Daddy*? This word elicited visions of tenderness, care, and love. For Flora, trusting God the Father had seemed impossible. But trusting a God that calls Himself "Daddy" was different.

Her new-found faith changed her life. She longed to tell everyone she met about her new "Daddy."

One rainy night after class, Flora missed the last bus home. "Now I'll have to wait forty-five minutes in this downpour," she grumbled. She glanced down at her watch—9:15 p.m. Looking up and down the empty street, she tried to spot a neon sign of an all-night diner or something—anything.

"I could probably wait inside the building." Flora glanced up in time to see the custodian locking the front doors. "Well, so much for that idea."

Flora barely noticed the first couple of times a dark-blue sedan drove by. But when it made a third pass, she turned and eyed the driver apprehensively. A feeling of panic forced her to look about for an escape should he prove dangerous.

The fourth time, the car stopped beside her. She whirled about and ran up the steps toward the locked doors.

She heard the car door opening. The driver shouted above the storm. "Miss le Fleur, it's me, Mr. Carter—your teacher." The man paused. "Did you miss the 9:15 bus?"

Flora turned and descended the steps. "I'm afraid I did."

"Do you live far from here?" he asked solicitously.

VICTORY OVER DEFEAT 93

"Yes." she replied. "But another bus should be along within the hour."

"You can't stand in this rain for an hour," he scolded. "Hop in. I'll take you home." Mr. Carter ran around the car to open the passenger door. "After all, it's partly my fault you missed the bus since class ran overtime."

Flora hopped into the car and adjusted her seatbelt.

Mr. Carter slipped behind the wheel. "Now, if you'll give me directions," he said, "I'll try to get you home before you catch pneumonia."

She gave him her address through chattering teeth.

He reached down and upped the heater control a notch. "I know the area. So relax and concentrate on getting warm."

As they rode, Mr. Carter made small talk, telling humorous anecdotes about his volunteer teaching experience. Before long, Flora relaxed enough to laugh at his humorous stories.

A block from Flora's apartment building, Mr. Carter stopped the car. She glanced over at the driver. "I live on the next block," she said.

"I know."

The click of the automatic door locks alerted Flora to danger. "I can get out here if you prefer," she added, trying to control her rising fear. "Please," she pleaded, "unlock the door."

"No!" The man leered at her as he spoke. "You aren't going anywhere until I say so."

"Please," she insisted.

"Stop playing games, Flora," the man growled. "You know what I want, and you want it too."

"No." Perspiration formed on Flora's forehead. "I don't. I thought you were being nice. You are my teacher."

Mr. Carter turned toward her, his arm on the back of the seat. "Come on, you Spanish girls do this all the time."

Tears welled up in Flora's eyes as she realized it was happening all over again. "No, this isn't possible," she breathed. "Tell me, Father, that this isn't happening again."

The man slid across the car seat. His fingers curled and uncurled as he ran them through the loose strand of hair at the back of her neck. "I've ached to see your beautiful hair flowing loose and free."

Turning toward her teacher, she pleaded, "Oh, Mr. Carter,

why you? I believed in you; trusted you." Flora buried her face in her hands, unaware she had spoken in English—clear, unaccented English!

"I can't believe this is happening," she sobbed, still speaking in the unfamiliar tongue. "I was six years old when my stepfather forced himself upon me." Flora related her story of suffering and abuse. She described the cruel beatings, Carlotta's curses, her brother-in-law's attempted rape—everything. "And then I found Jesus," she explained. "And for the first time, I felt clean and pure. I actually began to believe God could love someone like me—as a daughter, as a saint." Flora turned her face dejectedly toward the doorpost. "But maybe—maybe I was wrong. Maybe . . ."

Sometime during her story, Mr. Carter had returned to his own side of the car. He sat, leaning his forehead against the steering wheel. She glanced over at him, then continued. "Honest, Mr. Carter. I'm not the kind of girl you think I am." A warm peace filled her heart as she spoke. "I love my heavenly Father very much—more than life itself. So I can't do as you ask." She waited for a reply, but none came. Then all at once sobs escaped Mr. Carter as his shoulders heaved from a series of ragged shudders. "Flora, I beg you to forgive me for what I almost did tonight. I am so sorry. I-I-I did not know." He raised his head from the wheel. "You will forgive me, won't you?"

"Yes," Flora answered. "If I refused, God could not forgive my sins, could He?"

A click alerted Flora that Mr. Carter unlocked the car doors. Without delay she hopped from the car and ran down the street—free!

Once inside her apartment she shed her wet clothing and stepped into the shower. As the hot spray pelted her chilled body, Flora scrubbed herself in an effort to wash away the feeling of dirt and grime that engulfed her. She stayed in the shower until the hot spray turned tepid. Reluctantly, she toweled herself dry, slipped into a nightgown, and padded off to bed.

Sleep escaped her for some time, and whenever she closed her eyes, the faces from her past zoomed toward her at frightening speeds, threatening to crash into her.

Voices pummeled her from every side. "Soiled! Dirty! Cheap! Used!"

"It's your fault! You brought this on yourself. You're a meek, sniveling piece of trash!"

"You're no saint! That pure robe will never be yours!"

"You knew what I wanted! You wanted it too!"

The rest of the week, Flora worked at a frantic pace, in an effort to push the recurring nightmare from her mind. Tears streamed down her face as each night she read her paperback copy of *Steps to Christ*. She repeated again and again the comforting promises of forgiveness and hope she found in it.

She spent the next Sabbath alone in her apartment reading from the new Bible Pastor Torrez had given her. One by one, she looked up and claimed each text on forgiveness she found in the concordance. Then she read through the promises listed under "Father." Her favorite was Galatians 4:6.

As the sun set, the jangling telephone interrupted her study. It was Alejandra. "Hi, missed you at church today."

"Sorry. I had some thinking and praying to do, I guess."

"Something wrong?" Alejandra's voice betrayed her concern.

"It's a long story," Flora replied.

"How about doing something together tomorrow—maybe a picnic or something? We could pack a picnic lunch and walk to the little park next to that new church on Fourth Street."

"Sounds good. Around Ten?"

Flora was in the shower when Alejandra arrived the next morning. While drying her hair, she told her friend about the events of Wednesday night. "I'm sure Jesus put the words in my mouth for me to speak. All I know is, once I got started, I couldn't stop talking—in *English*!"

"Who would believe it?" Alejandra shook her head sadly. "Imagine. Mr. Carter!

"I should have known better than to get into the car with him in the first place," Flora lamented. "Will I ever learn not to be so trusting?"

"Don't put yourself down so much, Flora," Alejandra chided. "I probably would have made the same mistake under the circumstances."

At the park, the girls enjoyed looking at the tulips of various colors. When the bell in the church next to the park struck twelve noon, they decided to find a place to eat their lunch. They took a park bench on the opposite side of the church.

As they passed the building, Flora glanced up toward the people leaving the sanctuary. Suddenly her heart leaped to her throat. Trembling, she pointed toward the pastor.

There stood Mr. Carter, her teacher, garbed in the robes of a minister, shaking hands with his parishioners!

Before Flora could escape, Mr. Carter glanced her way. Their eyes met. Tangled messages of fear, shame, shock, and discovery held them both spellbound for several seconds.

"Let's get out of here," Alejandra whispered, driving Flora from the scene. "I can't believe it—Mr. Carter, a minister?"

As the girls reached her apartment, Flora turned toward her friend and announced, "You know, God has been giving me the power to become His daughter all along, just like Pastor Torrez said."

Alejandra stared at her friend. "What brought that on?"

"For a long time, I resented the Power I supposedly possessed. I even hated it at times. Now I realize it was that Power that helped me survive the terrible experiences I have gone through. It was that Power that saved me from being raped last Wednesday night." Flora paused. "That Power has enabled me to become a saint—and now, to live as a saint. Isn't that exciting?"

"Have you ever considered that the Lord may have used you to reach Mr. Carter?"

"Oh no, not me. I don't feel . . ." Flora stopped midsentence, her brow knitted. She remembered Pastor Torrez's words. "One does not have to feel saintly to be a saint. It is your faith in God, not your feelings that guarantees your place in God's family." Suddenly she realized God had worked through her to help Mr. Carter—like Señor Ortega had helped her so many years before.

Reaching for her Bible Flora said, "I may not have my doctor-husband, but I have a Bible of my very own, and God has given me the power to become His daughter—one of His saints!" An unexpected bubble of happiness burst from the delighted young woman. "My first assignment as a saint . . . ," she thought as she caught a glimpse of herself in the mirror above her bureau. She straightened her shoulders and smiled. She saw a vibrant young woman smile back at her, not the cringing victim of others' sins and lusts, but the legitimate daughter of the Most High—endowed with all the Power the position entailed.